History of England

History of England

A Concise Outline

Jack J. Kański

Copyright © 2018 Jack J. Kański

The moral right of the author has been asserted.

Apart from any fair dealing for the purposes of research or private study, or criticism or review, as permitted under the Copyright, Designs and Patents Act 1988, this publication may only be reproduced, stored or transmitted, in any form or by any means, with the prior permission in writing of the publishers, or in the case of reprographic reproduction in accordance with the terms of licences issued by the Copyright Licensing Agency. Enquiries concerning reproduction outside those terms should be sent to the publishers.

Matador
9 Priory Business Park,
Wistow Road, Kibworth Beauchamp,
Leicestershire. LE8 0RX
Tel: 0116 279 2299
Email: books@troubador.co.uk
Web: www.troubador.co.uk/matador
Twitter: @matadorbooks

ISBN 978 1788035 668

British Library Cataloguing in Publication Data.
A catalogue record for this book is available from the British Library.

Printed and bound by CPI Group (UK) Ltd, Croydon, CR0 4YY
Typeset in 11pt Minion Pro by Troubador Publishing Ltd, Leicester, UK

Matador is an imprint of Troubador Publishing Ltd

To Dafydd and Celia

PREFACE

The main purpose of this book is to present the history of England in a concise and didactic way. For this purpose I have used a bullet-point format with many illustrations, so as to enable the reader to absorb the text more easily. The two last chapters describe important political and military personalities.

I am very grateful to Tom Ayling for reviewing the manuscript and for making many helpful suggestions. I have relied on Wikipedia for core text material and on Google for the images.

CONTENTS

EARLY INVASIONS   1
    ROMAN   2
    ANGLO-SAXON   3
    VIKING   4

HOUSE OF NORMANDY   7
    KING WILLIAM 1st (THE CONQUEROR)   8
    KING WILLIAM 2nd (RUFUS)   11
    KING HENRY 1st   12
    KING STEPHEN   13

HOUSE OF PLANTAGENET   15
    KING HENRY 2nd   16
    KING RICHARD 1st (LION HEART)   18
    KING JOHN   20
    Prince Llywelyn (the Great)   22
    KING HENRY 3rd   23
    KING EDWARD 1st   24
    William Wallace   26
    Robert (the Bruce)   27

KING EDWARD 2nd	28
KING EDWARD 3rd	30
Prince John of Gaunt	32
KING RICHARD 2nd	33
KING HENRY 4th	34
Prince Owen Glendower	35
KING HENRY 5th	36
KING HENRY 6th	38
KING EDWARD 4th	40
KING RICHARD 3rd	42

HOUSE OF TUDOR — 45

KING HENRY 7th	46
KING HENRY 8th	48
Cardinal Wolsey	52
Thomas Cromwell	53
Thomas More	54
KING EDWARD 6th	55
QUEEN MARY 1st TUDOR	58
QUEEN ELIZABETH 1st	59

HOUSE OF STUART — 63

KING JAMES 1st	64
KING CHARLES 1st	66
Civil Wars	68
Oliver Cromwell	70

KING CHARLES 2nd	71
KING JAMES 2nd	74
KING WILLIAM 3rd AND QUEEN MARY 2nd	76
Jacobite Uprisings	78
QUEEN ANNE	78
Acts of Union	79

HOUSE OF HANOVER 81

KING GEORGE 1st	82
KING GEORGE 2nd	84
KING GEORGE 3rd	86
Industrial Revolution	88
KING GEORGE 4th	89
KING WILLIAM 4th	91
QUEEN VICTORIA	93

HOUSE OF SAXE-COBURG AND GOTHA 97

KING EDWARD 7th	98

HOUSE OF WINDSOR 103

First World War	104
KING GEORGE 5th	106
KING EDWARD 8th	108
KING GEORGE 6th	110
Second World War	112
QUEEN ELIZABETH 2nd	113

POLITICIANS 117

ROBERT WALPOLE, 1st EARL OF ORFORD	118
THOMAS PELHAM-HOLLES, 1st DUKE OF NEWCASTLE	119
WILLIAM PITT (THE ELDER), 1st EARL OF CHATHAM	120
AUGUSTUS FITZROY, 3rd DUKE OF GRAFTON	121
FREDERICK NORTH, 2nd EARL OF GUILDFORD (LORD NORTH)	122
WILLIAM PITT (THE YOUNGER)	123
SPENCER PERCEVAL	125
ROBERT JENKINSON, 2nd EARL OF LIVERPOOL	126
GEORGE CANNING	127
ARTHUR WELLESLEY, 1st DUKE OF WELLINGTON	128
WILLIAM LAMB, 2nd VISCOUNT MELBOURNE	129
SIR ROBERT PEEL, 2nd BARONET	130
JOHN RUSSELL, 1st EARL RUSSELL	131
EDWARD SMITH-STANLEY, 14th EARL OF DERBY	132
HENRY JOHN TEMPLE, 3rd VISCOUNT PALMERSTON	133
BENJAMIN DISRAELI, 1st EARL OF BEACONSFIELD	134
WILLIAM GLADSTONE	135
ROBERT GASCOYNE-CECIL, 3rd MARQUESS OF SALISBURY	136
ARTHUR BALFOUR, 1st EARL OF BALFOUR	137
HENRY CAMPBELL-BANNERMAN	138
EDWARD GREY, 1st VISCOUNT GREY OF FALLODON	139
H. H. ASQUITH, 1st EARL OF OXFORD AND ASQUITH	140

DAVID LLOYD GEORGE, 1st EARL LLOYD-GEORGE OF DWYFOR	141
RAMSAY MACDONALD	142
STANLEY BALDWIN, 1st EARL BALDWIN OF BEWDLEY	143
NEVILLE CHAMBERLAIN	145
EDWARD WOOD, 1st EARL OF HALIFAX	146
WINSTON CHURCHILL	147
CLEMENT ATTLEE, 1st EARL ATTLEE	149
ANTHONY EDEN, 1st EARL OF AVON	150
HAROLD MACMILLAN, 1st EARL OF STOCKTON	151
HAROLD WILSON, BARON OF RIEVAULX	153
EDWARD HEATH	154
MARGARET THATCHER, BARONESS THATCHER OF KESTEVEN	155
TONY BLAIR	157

MILITARY COMMANDERS   159

JOHN CHURCHILL, 1st DUKE OF MARLBOROUGH	160
HORATIO NELSON, 1st VISCOUNT NELSON	162
ARTHUR WELLESLEY, 1st DUKE OF WELLINGTON	164
CHARLES GORDON	166
HERBERT KITCHENER, 1st EARL KITCHENER	168
EDMUND ALLENBY, 1st VISCOUNT ALLENBY	170
JOHN FRENCH, 1st EARL OF YPRES	171
DOUGLAS HAIG, 1st EARL HAIG	173
HUGH TRENCHARD, 1st VISCOUNT TRENCHARD	174

JOHN JELLICOE, 1st EARL JELLICOE	176
DAVID BEATTY, 1st EARL BEATTY	177
ARTHUR TEDDER, 1st BARON TEDDER	178
HUGH DOWDING, 1st BARON DOWDING	179
ARTHUR HARRIS, 1st BARONET	180
ANDREW CUNNINGHAM, 1st VISCOUNT CUNNINGHAM OF HYNDHOPE	181
LOUIS MOUNTBATTEN, 1st EARL MOUNTBATTEN OF BURMA	182
HAROLD ALEXANDER, 1st EARL ALEXANDER OF TUNIS	183
BERNARD MONTGOMERY, 1st VISCOUNT MONTGOMERY OF ALAMEIN	184
ARCHIBALD WAVELL, 1st EARL WAVELL	187

1
EARLY INVASIONS

ROMAN

- Before the Roman invasion, Britain was ruled by tribes of people called the Celts.
- In 55 BC, Julius Caesar invaded Britain but was unable to establish a province.
- In 43 AD, the Romans conquered Britain, at the behest of the **Emperor Claudius.**
- In 60 AD, warrior–queen Boudicca (Fig. 1.1) rose against the occupying Roman forces but was defeated.

(Fig 1.1)

ANGLO-SAXON

- From the middle of the 4th century, England was progressively settled by Germanic groups known as the *Anglo-Saxons*, consisting of Angles and Saxons from what is now the Danish/German border area, and Jutes from the Jutland peninsula (Fig. 1.2).
- The indigenous Britons were invaded by *Picts,* from the north (now Scotland) and the *Scotti* (now Ireland).
- The Saxons established seven kingdoms: *Sussex, Kent, Essex, Mercia, East Anglia, Northumbria,* and *Wessex* (Fig. 1.3).
- Mercian power reached its peak under **King Offa**, and after his death in 796, Wessex became the strongest kingdom under **King Egbert.**
- The Anglo-Saxons, including *Saxonified* Britons, progressively spread into England, by a combination of military conquest and cultural assimilation.

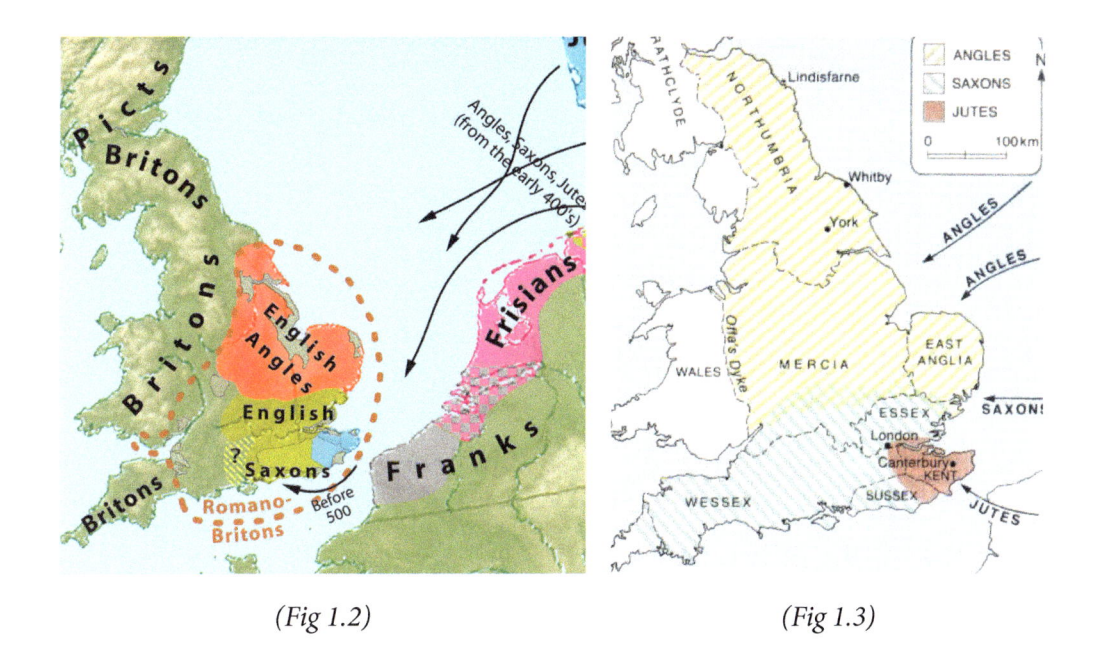

(Fig 1.2) *(Fig 1.3)*

VIKING

- In 793, the Vikings (Figs. 1.4 and 1.5) attacked the monastery of Lindisfarne; in 867, Northumbria, and in 869, East Anglia, also fell.

(Fig 1.4)

(Fig 1.5)

Early Invasions | 5

- In May 878, **King Alfred the Great of Wessex** (Fig. 1.6) defeated the Danes, and his success was sustained by his son **King Edward the Elder** (Fig. 1.7), who incorporated Mercia and East Anglia.
- Edward's son **King Æthelstan** extended the borders of Wessex northwards and in 917, conquered the Kingdom of York and invaded Scotland.

(Fig 1.6)   *(Fig 1.7)*

- In 978, with the accession of **King Æthelred the Unready,** the Danish threat resurfaced, when **King Harold Bluetooth** and later his son, **King Sweyn,** launched devastating invasions.
- Anglo–Saxon forces were resoundingly defeated and King Æthelred grew increasingly desperate; for almost 20 years he managed to keep the Danes away from the English coasts by paying them increasingly large sums of money but in 1002, he ordered the massacre of all the Danes in England.
- In anger, Sweyn unleashed a decade of devastating attacks, seized the throne but died in 1014 AD.
- Æthelred recovered the throne but died suddenly in 1016.
- Sweyn's son, **Cnut** killed Æthelred's son, **King Edmund 2nd Ironside,** and became **King Cnut of England** (Fig. 1.8).
- Under Cnut's rule, England became the centre of government for an empire which also included Denmark, Norway and a part of Sweden (Fig. 1.9).

- Cnut was succeeded by his sons, but in 1042 AD, the native dynasty was restored with the accession of **King Edward the Confessor** (Fig. 1.10).

(Fig 1.8)

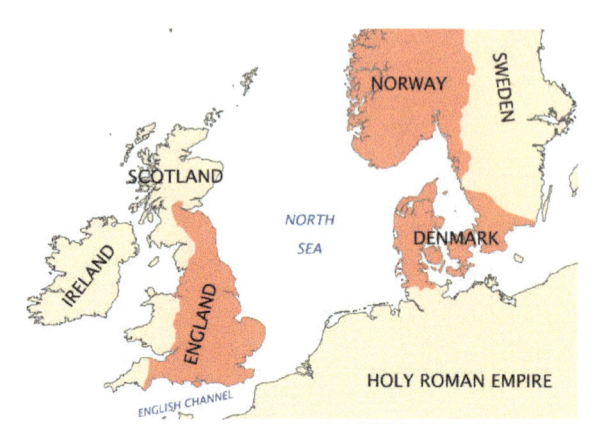

(Fig 1.9)

(Fig 1.10)

2
HOUSE OF NORMANDY

KING WILLIAM 1st (THE CONQUEROR)

(Fig. 2.1)

- William (1027–1087) was *Duke of Normandy* (1035–1087) and *King of England* (1066–1087); he was the illegitimate son of Robert 1st Duke of Normandy and his mistress, Herleva.
- In 1053, he married **Matilda of Flanders** (Fig. 2.2) and had 10 children including; **Robert Curthose, William 2nd, Henry 1st**, and **Adela,** the mother of **King Stephen**.

(Fig 2.2)

- William was tall, red–haired, brave, strong, just and pious but also ruthless in war.
- In 1066, he invaded England in a campaign known as the Norman Conquest and defeated the Saxons under **King Harold 2nd Godwinson**, at the *Battle of Hastings* (Fig. 2.3), during which Harold was killed.
- William was crowned king at Westminster Abbey (Fig. 2.4), but by 1067 he faced revolts. He spent four years brutally crushing each one and forced Scotland and Wales to recognise him as overlord.

(Fig 2.3)   (Fig 2.4)

- William ordered the compilation of the Domesday Book, a survey of the entire population and their property for tax purposes.
- The King built many castles including those at: Warwick, Nottingham, Lincoln, York, and the White Tower of the Tower of London; he also built many cathedrals including that at Ely.
- By about 1072, England was conquered (Fig. 2.5) and William spent the remainder of his reign in France campaigning against **King Philip 1st** and the **Counts of Flanders** and **Anjou.**
- On his deathbed, William is supposed to have left the English crown to his third son, **William**, Normandy to his eldest son, **Robert**

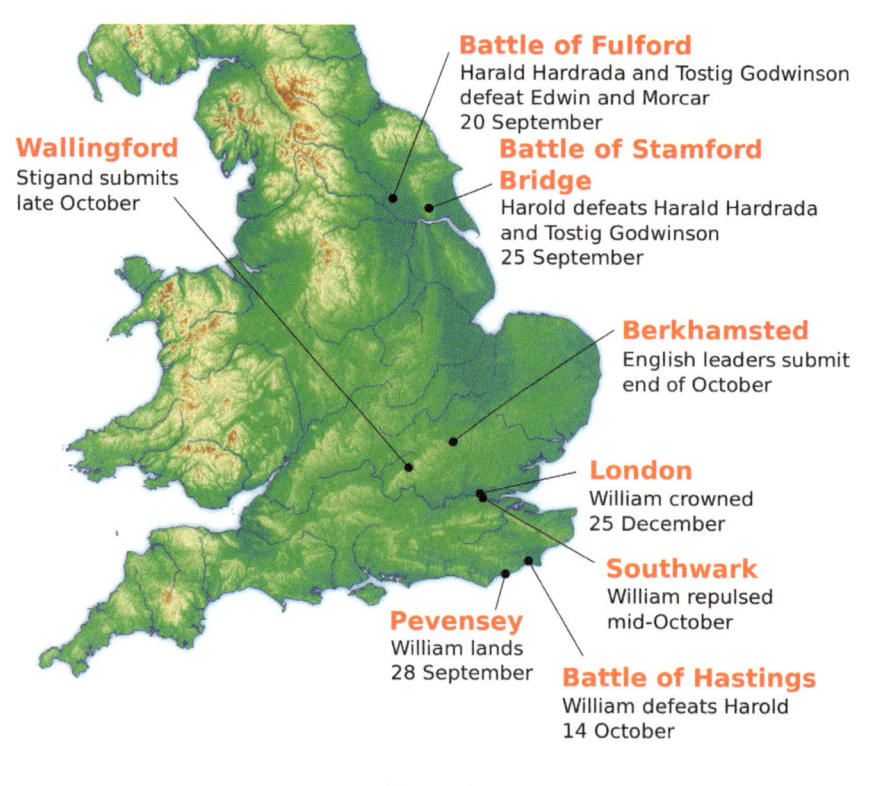

Battle of Fulford
Harald Hardrada and Tostig Godwinson defeat Edwin and Morcar
20 September

Wallingford
Stigand submits late October

Battle of Stamford Bridge
Harold defeats Harald Hardrada and Tostig Godwinson
25 September

Berkhamsted
English leaders submit end of October

London
William crowned 25 December

Southwark
William repulsed mid-October

Pevensey
William lands 28 September

Battle of Hastings
William defeats Harold 14 October

(Fig 2.5)

Curthose, but **Henry,** his fourth son, was left no land but a monetary compensation; his second son **Richard** died young.
- In 1087, King William 1st died in a riding accident aged 59.
- The immediate consequence of William's death was war between his sons, Robert and William, over control of England and Normandy; he was eventually succeeded by William who became William 2nd Rufus.

KING WILLIAM 2nd (RUFUS)

(Fig 2.6)

- William (1056–1100) was *King of England* (1087–1100) with powers in *Normandy* and influence in *Scotland*; he was the third son of William 1st and Matilda of Flanders.
- He was called 'Rufus' because of the redness of his face.
- He was a very bad king who plundered churches and was ruthless, greedy and cruel.
- He was a tyrant with savage and arbitrary laws (Forest laws).
- William managed to keep the peace and successfully suppressed two rebellions.
- In 1100, aged 42, he was killed by an arrow while hunting in the New Forest (Fig. 2.7).
- As he did not marry and had no issue, he nominated his older brother Robert as his heir but was succeeded by his other brother who became Henry 1st.

(Fig 2.7)

KING HENRY 1st

(Fig. 2.8)

- Henry (1068–1135), was *King of England* (1100–1135) and *Duke of Normandy* (1106–1135); he was the fourth son of William 1st and Matilda of Flanders.
- Henry was married twice; first to **Matilda of Scotland** and then to **Adeliza of Louvain.**
- He was well educated and was known as '*Henry Beauclerc*' (good writer).
- Henry could be harsh to the point of savagery, but he inspired loyalty, was clever, and capable; he established knights and chivalry.
- Henry was present at the fatal hunting party in the New Forest, where his brother **King William 2nd (Rufus)** was killed, and almost before the King drew his last breath, Henry galloped to nearby Winchester and seized the throne, before his older brother Robert's imminent return from the Crusades.
- Henry's reign was long and successful; he worked hard to reform the country and smooth the differences between the Anglo–Saxon and Anglo–Norman societies.
- In 1101, his brother, Robert, invaded England to dispute Henry's control, but the two came to an amicable agreement that confirmed Henry as king.

- In 1105, Henry, in turn, invaded Normandy and defeated Robert, keeping him prisoner for the rest of his life.
- Henry had four legitimate children, of which only **Matilda** survived; she later married the future Holy Roman Emperor, Henry 5th, and became an Empress.
- The death by drowning of his only son and heir, William Adelin, caused problems regarding succession.
- Henry decided that his daughter **Empress Matilda** (same name as her mother) should succeed him, but after his death, the barons ignored his wishes and supported his nephew **Stephen of Blois**.
- In 1135, the King died in Normandy, aged 67, after overindulging in eating lampreys; he was succeeded by his nephew who became King Stephen.

KING STEPHEN

(Fig 2.7)

- Stephen of Blois (1096–1154) was *King of England* (1135–1154) and *Count of Boulogne*; he was the son of Stephen Count of Blois and Adela of Normandy, daughter of William 1st.
- Stephen married **Matilda of Boulogne** (Fig. 2.10), and they had five children.

- The king was charming, genial, dashing and brave but he was also unreliable.
- **Empress Matilda** (Fig. 2.11), daughter of Henry 1st, contested the crown and this led to the Civil War from 1139–1153, the period known as the 'Anarchy'.
- In 1139, Empress Matilda invaded England with her illegitimate half-brother, **Robert of Gloucester**; King Stephen was captured, and Matilda was proclaimed Queen.
- Stephen's wife, **Queen Matilda**, brought about his release and Empress Matilda, escaped to France.
- Stephen effectively reigned unopposed until his death in 1154; he had no heirs and was the last of the Norman kings.
- When Stephen's son and heir apparent, Eustace, predeceased him in 1153, the King reached an accommodation with **Henry of Anjou** to succeed him.
- In 1154, the King died from dysentery, aged 58, to be succeeded by Henry 2nd.

3
HOUSE OF PLANTAGENET

KING HENRY 2nd

(Fig 3.1)

- Henry Curtmantle (1133–1189), also known as Henry Plantagenet, was *King of England* (1154–1189); he also ruled as *Count of Anjou, Count of Maine, Duke of Normandy, Duke of Aquitaine,* and *Lord of Ireland.*
- He also controlled Wales, Scotland and Brittany at various times; he was the son of Geoffrey 5th of Anjou and Empress Matilda, daughter of Henry 1st.
- Henry married **Eleanor of Aquitaine** (Fig. 3.2), whose previous marriage to King Louis 7th of France had been annulled.
- Henry and Eleanor had seven children, including two future kings: Richard 1st and John.
- Henry was an extraordinary man, who achieved a lot during his 35-year reign; he ruled England and much of France, (*'Angevin Empire'.*)

House of Plantagenet | 17

(Fig 3.2)

- In 1173, war broke out between Henry and his sons, encouraged by **Queen Eleanor**, about who should inherit which part of Henry's Empire.
- Eleanor outlived her husband and saw two of her sons on the throne.
- **Thomas Becket** (Archbishop of Canterbury) became the King's chancellor and dearest friend, but later he became his bitterest enemy and was murdered in *Canterbury* by four of Henry's knights (Fig. 3.3).

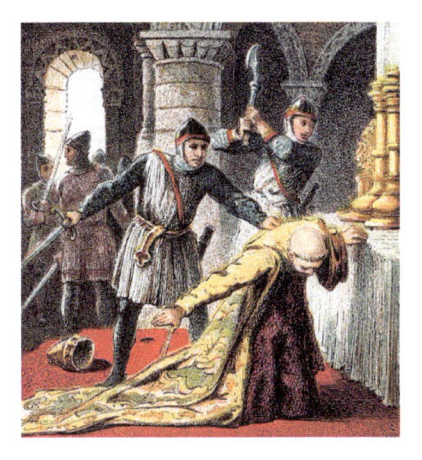

(Fig 3.3)

- In 1189, Henry was defeated by his son, **Richard,** who was supported by **King Philip 2nd Augustus of France**.
- Henry agreed to guarantee the crown to Richard. Henry also discovered that his favourite youngest son, John, had joined the alliance against him.
- The King died aged 56 and was succeeded by his son who became Richard 1st.

KING RICHARD 1st (LION HEART)

(Fig. 3.4)

- Richard (1157–1199), also known as the 'Lion Heart', was *King of England* (1189–1199) and also ruled at various times *as Duke of Normandy, Duke of Aquitaine,* and *Count of Anjou*; he was the son of Henry 2nd and Eleanor of Aquitaine.
- In 1191, Richard married **Berengaria of Navarre**, but they had no children.

- He was also known as *'The Absent King'* because he was preoccupied with foreign wars, and spent much time defending his French territories.
- The King's main interest was to raise money for a new crusade, and to this end he cancelled the *Treaty of Falaise*, under which the Scots recognised English over-lordship, in return for a substantial sum of money.

(Fig 3.5)

- In 1191, during the Third Crusade, he defeated **Saladin** at the *Battle of Arsuf* (Fig. 3.5) but failed to take Jerusalem.
- In 1192, he was captured and imprisoned by **Holy Emperor Henry 6th** but freed the next year following payment of a ransom.
- In 1199, Richard died in France, aged 41, from a wound inflicted by a crossbow bolt that became gangrenous.
- He was succeeded by his brother who became King John.

KING JOHN

(Fig. 3.6)

- John Lackland (1167–1216) was *King of England* (1119–1216); he was the youngest of five sons by Henry 2nd and Eleanor of Aquitaine.
- John was married twice; first to **Isabel of Gloucester** with whom he had no children, and then to **Isabella of Angouleme**, with whom he had five.
- John lost most of the Duchy of Normandy to **King Philip 2nd**, and this resulted in the collapse of most of the Angevin Empire, and following the disastrous *Battle of Bouvines* (1214), he was forced to accept unfavourable peace terms with France.
- John clashed with the church and was excommunicated from 1209 to 1213.
- Over the course of his reign, a combination of higher taxes and unsuccessful wars made John unpopular with his barons, and in 1215, some of them rebelled.

- John met their leaders at Runnymede in June 1215 to seal the *Great Charter* (Magna Carta) (Fig. 3.7), which imposed legal limits on the king's personal powers.

(Fig. 3.7)

- Because he had signed and sealed the Marna Carta under duress, John received approval from the Pope to break his word as soon as hostilities had ceased, thus provoking the *First Barons' War* and an invited French invasion by **Prince Louis of France.**
- John travelled around the country to oppose the rebel forces, directing a two-month siege of the rebel-held Rochester Castle.
- In 1216, aged 49, the King died suddenly following a violent gastric upset, to be succeeded by his nine-year-old son who became Henry 3rd.

Prince Llywelyn (the Great)

(Fig. 3.8)

- Llywelyn the Great (1172–1240) was a *Prince of Gwynedd* and eventually *de facto* ruler over most of Wales for 45 years.
- By 1200, he was sole ruler of Gwynedd and married **Joan,** the daughter of **King John of England**; the relations between Llywelyn and John remained good until 1200 when John invaded Gwynedd.
- Llywelyn was forced to give up all lands west of the River Conwy but was able to recover them the following year in alliance with the other Welsh princes.
- In 1215, he allied himself with the barons who forced John to sign the Magna Carta.
- Following King John's death, Llywelyn concluded the *Treaty of Worcester* with his successor, Henry 3rd.
- In 1218, the *Peace of Middle* marked the end of Llywelyn's military career, but he maintained his position in Wales until his death in 1240.

KING HENRY 3rd

(Fig. 3.9)

- Henry of Winchester (1207–1272) was *King of England, Lord of Ireland* and *Duke of Aquitaine* (1216–1272); he was son of King John and Isabella of Angouleme.
- Henry married **Eleanor of Province** with whom he had nine children.
- Henry was only nine years old when his father died and the regents during his years of minority were **William Marshall** (1st Earl of Pembroke) and **Hubert de Burgh** (1st Earl of Kent).
- Henry was a weak king lacking military prowess and spent much of his reign fighting the barons over the Magna Carta.
- His reign was punctuated by numerous rebellions and civil wars, often provoked by incompetence and his over-reliance on French courtiers.
- **Simon de Montfort** (Fig. 3.10), a Frenchman, was made Earl of Leicester, and then married the King's sister without his permission.

(Fig. 3.10)

24 | History of England

- Simon de Montfort rebelled, and captured Henry and his son **Prince Edward** (later Edward 1st) at the *Battle of Lewes* (1264), and the King was reduced to a mere figurehead.
- Subsequently, Prince Edward escaped from capture and killed de Montfort at the *Battle of Evesham* (1265) (Fig. 3.11).
- In 1272, the King died aged 65 of ill-health, to be succeeded by his son, the future Edward 1st.

(Fig. 3.11)

KING EDWARD 1st

(Fig. 3.12)

House of Plantagenet | 25

- Edward Longshanks (1239–1307) was *King of England* (1272–1307); he was the son of Henry 3rd and Eleanor of Province.
- He was married twice, first **Eleanor of Castile** (Figure 3.12) and then to **Margaret of France.**
- Edward was tall, strong, handsome, gallant and chivalrous. He enacted numerous laws strengthening the powers of his government, and he summoned the first officially sanctioned Parliament of England.
- In 1284, by the *Statute of Wales*, the principality was finally annexed and, as a gesture of reconciliation, the King's new born son was proclaimed 'Prince of Wales', and the title has been held by successive heirs to the throne ever since.
- Edward conquered Scotland (Hammer of the Scots) and chose **John Balliol** as king (puppet) and then removed him from the throne.
- In 1296 and 1298 he defeated **William Wallace** (later executed) and the Scottish Coronation Stone of Scone (Fig. 3.13) was taken to Westminster Abbey where it remained for 700 years.
- Scottish resistance, however, continued and Edward fought a costly and drawn-out campaign against **Robert the Bruce,** King of the Scots**.**
- In 1307, the King died aged 68, to be succeeded by his fourth son who became Edward 2nd.

(Fig. 3.13)

William Wallace

(Fig. 3.14)

- Sir William Wallace (1270–1305) was a Scottish knight who became one of the main leaders during the *Wars of Scottish Independence.*
- In September 1297, **Wallace** and **Andrew Moray** defeated an English army at the *Battle of Sterling Bridge.*
- He was appointed Guardian of Scotland and served until his defeat at the *Battle of Falkirk* (July 1298).
- In August 1305, Wallace was captured and handed over to **King Edward 1st of England** who had him tried (Fig. 3.15) and then hanged, drawn, and quartered for high treason and crimes against English civilians.
- Since his death, Wallace has obtained an iconic status far beyond his homeland.

(Fig. 3.15)

Robert (the Bruce)

(Fig. 3.16)

- Robert (1st) the Bruce (1274–1329) was *King of the Scots* (1306– 1329), who fought successfully to regain Scotland's place as an independent country and is today revered in Scotland as a national hero.
- As Earl of Carrick he took part in **William Wallace's** revolt against **King Edward 1st of England**.
- In March 1306 Bruce was crowned King of Scots, and the following year, he defeated an English army at the *Battle of Loundon Hill* and waged a highly successful guerrilla war against the English.
- A series of military victories between 1310 and 1314 won him control of much of Scotland, and at the *Battle of Bannockburn* (1314) (Fig. 3.17), Robert defeated a much larger English army under **King Edward 2nd of England**, and re-established an independent Scottish kingdom, but despite this, Edward 2nd refused to renounce his claim to the over-lordship of Scotland.
- In 1324, the Pope recognised Robert 1st as king of an independent Scotland.
- In 1327, the English deposed Edward 2nd in favour of his son, Edward 3rd, and peace was concluded between Scotland and England with the *Treaty of Edinburgh-Northampton*, by which Edward 3rd renounced all claims to sovereignty over Scotland.

(Fig. 3.17)

KING EDWARD 2nd

(Fig. 3.18)

- Edward of Caernarfon (1284–1327) was *King of England* (1307–1327); he was the fourth son of Edward 1st and Eleanor of Castile.
- Edward married **Isabella of France** daughter of **King Philip 4th** and had five children.
- He exhibited self-indulgence and lacked judgement in his private life.

- He preferred to engage in thatching and boat–building rather than jousting and hunting, and his weakness brought the monarchy to the brink of disaster.
- Edward spent most of his reign trying in vain to control the nobility, who in return showed him continual hostility.
- **King Robert the Bruce** began retaking previously conquered territory, and easily defeated the English army at the *Battle of Bannockburn* (1314) thus ensuring Scottish independence for a further three centuries.
- Edward showered favours on his companion, **Piers Gaveston** (Fig. 3.19), with whom he might have had a homosexual relationship, and in 1312, the King's enemies, including his cousin, **Thomas of Lancaster**, captured and murdered Gaveston.
- In 1326, Edward's wife, **Queen Isabella**, fled to France, and then with her lover, **Roger Mortimer**, invaded England and deposed the King.
- In 1327, Edward abdicated, and a few months later he was murdered aged 43, and was succeeded by his son who became Edward 3rd.

(Fig. 3.19)

KING EDWARD 3rd

(Fig. 3.20)

- Edward (1312–1377) was *King of England* (1327–1377); he was the son of Edward 2nd and Isabella of France.
- He married **Phillippa of Hainault** with whom he had 13 children, of whom six were sons, notably **Edward the Black Prince** (Fig. 3.21) and **John of Gaunt**; the former predeceased him.
- Edward excelled at jousting and was affable, sporting and brave; he instituted the *Order of the Garter* and was keen on heraldry.
- He was crowned at age 14 after his father was deposed by his mother, **Isabella**, and her lover, **Roger Mortimer**.

(Fig. 3.21)

- Aged 17, he led a successful coup against Mortimer, the *de facto* ruler of the country, and began his personal reign; Mortimer was seized (Fig. 3.22) and executed and his mother retired.

(Fig. 3.22)

- Edward's reign restored royal authority and transformed England into the most efficient military power in Europe.
- After defeating, but not subjugating, the Kingdom of Scotland, he declared himself heir to the French throne in 1338, but his claim was denied and the *Hundred Years' War* ensued.
- The war went well for England with victories at the *Battle* of *Crecy* (1346) Fig. (3.23) and the *Battle of Poitiers* (1356) leading to the highly favourable *Treaty of Brétigny*.

(Fig. 3.23)

- Edward's later years were marked by international failure and domestic strife.
- In 1377, the King died aged 64, to be succeeded by his grandson who became Richard 2nd.

Prince John of Gaunt

(Fig. 3.24)

- John of Gaunt (1st Duke of Lancaster) (1340–1399) was the third of five surviving sons of King Edward 3rd of England and Phillipa of Hainault; he was called '*John of Gaunt*' because he was born in Ghent then rendered in English as *Gaunt*.
- As a younger brother of the Prince of Wales (Edward the Black Prince), John exercised great influence over the English throne during the minority of Edward's son, who became **King Richard 2nd**.
- His legitimate Lancastrian male heirs include **Kings Henry 4th, Henry 5th** and **Henry 6th.**
- His eldest son and heir, **Henry Bolingbroke** (later Henry 4th) was exiled for ten years by **King Richard 2nd** and when John of Gaunt died in 1399, his estates and titles were declared forfeit to the crown, since King Richard 2nd had named Henry a traitor and changed his sentence to exile for life.
- Subsequently, however, Henry Bolingbroke returned from exile, deposed Richard 2nd and reigned as King Henry 4th of England (1399–1413).

KING RICHARD 2nd

(Fig. 3.25)

- Richard of Bordeaux (1367–1400) was *King of England* (1377–1399); he was the younger son of Edward Prince of Wales ('Black Prince') and Joan of Kent.
- He was married twice, first to **Anne of Bohemia,** and then to **Isabella of Valois;** both marriages were childless.
- Richard was aged 10 years when he became king and initially the country was run by a regency under his uncle **John of Gaunt.**
- John of Gaunt was the father of the future **King Henry 4th**, and the third son of **King Edward 3rd**, and had some claim to the throne himself.
- Richard was defeated at the *Battle of Radcot Bridge* (1387), outside Oxford, by **Henry Bolingbroke**, his cousin, and the son of John of Gaunt.
- Subsequently Richard regained power and banished Henry into exile in France.
- **Henry** returned to England and captured **Richard**, who was forced to abdicate.
- In 1399, Richard died in captivity aged 33 and was succeeded by his first cousin, Henry Bolingbroke who became King Henry 4th.

KING HENRY 4th

(Fig. 3.26)

- Henry Bolingbroke (1367–1413) was *King of England* (1399–1413) and *Lord of Ireland* (1399–1413); he was the son of John of Gaunt and Blanche of Lancaster.
- Henry was married twice, first to **Mary de Bohun**, with whom he had seven children, and then a childless marriage to **Joanna of Navarre**.
- Although Henry had a dubious ascent to the throne, he was a dynamic king.
- Not only was he athletic and liked jousting, he also liked the arts.
- Henry was highly religious and had been on a pilgrimage to Jerusalem.
- Throughout his reign, he was dogged by the fact that others had a better claim to the throne, and he had to deal with various rebellions and uprisings.
- In 1400, the Welsh, under **Owen Glendower** (Owain Glyndwr), pushed the English forces back to the borders and fighting went on for nine years.
- In 1403, **Sir Henry Percy** (Hotspur), son of the Earl of Northumberland, rebelled and was killed at the *Battle of Shrewsbury* (Fig. 3.27).
- In 1405, the Earl of Northumberland himself rebelled in alliance with Glendower and Scrope (Archbishop of York), but they were defeated and the archbishop was executed.

(Fig. 3.27)

- In 1408, the **Earl of Northumberland** launched another rebellion but was defeated and killed in battle.
- Henry became tired and unwell and had to rely on the Council for day-to-day government and, shortly before his death, he developed a debilitating skin disease.
- In 1414, the King died aged 46, to be succeeded by his son who became Henry 5th.

Prince Owen Glendower

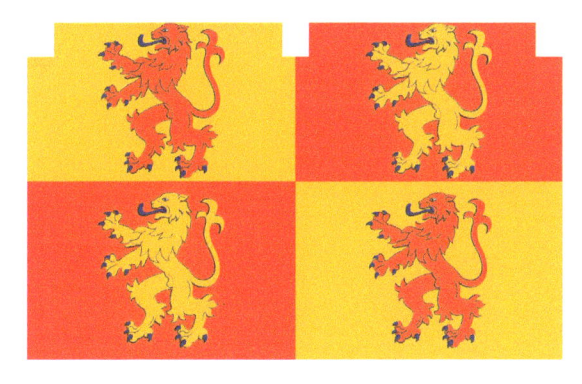

(Fig. 3.28)

- Owen Glendower (Owain Glyndŵr) (1359–1415) was the last native Welshman to hold the title *Prince of Wales*, and instigated a fierce and long-running, but ultimately unsuccessful, revolt against English rule.
- On 16 September, 1400, Glendower instigated the Welsh revolt against **King Henry 4th of England**.
- The uprising was initially successful and he rapidly gained control of large areas of Wales, but eventually the revolt was suppressed by the superior resources of the English.
- In 1409, Glendower was driven from his last strongholds but he avoided capture and the last documented sighting of him was in 1412.
- He twice ignored offers of a pardon from the new **King Henry 5th of England**, and despite the large rewards offered, he was never betrayed.

KING HENRY 5th

(Fig. 3.29)

- Henry (1387–1422) was *King of England* (1413–1422); he was the son of Henry 4th and Mary de Bohun.
- He married **Catherine of Valois** with whom he had a son.
- Henry was the last of the great warrior kings of the Middle Ages, and during his short reign, he expanded England's territory in France, became heir to the French throne.
- On succeeding to the throne, he pardoned his father's enemies, but

- he renewed hostilities with France and began military campaigns which were considered to be a new phase of the *Hundred Years' War*, referred to as the *Lancastrian War*.
- Henry won several notable victories over the French, including at the *Battle of Agincourt* (1415) (Fig. 3.30).

(Fig. 3.30)

- In 1420, according to the *Treaty of Troyes*, he became regent of France and heir to the throne of the current **King of France Charles 6th.**
- The Treaty also provided that he would marry Charles' daughter, **Catherine of Valois**.
- They married in 1421, but in the following year, Henry died in France of dysentery aged 35 and was succeeded by his son, who became Henry 6th.

KING HENRY 6th

(Fig. 3.31)

- Henry (1421–1471) was *King of England* (1422–1461 and 1470–1471); he was the only son of King Henry 5th and Catherine of Valois.
- Unlike his father, Henry showed no interest in war but had a passion for religion.
- He married **Margaret of Anjou** with whom he had one son.
- Henry became king as a nine-month-old baby, and while he was growing up, England was ruled by the Regency Council of England (1422–1437) until he became of age.
- The Council attempted to install him to the French throne according to the *Treaty of Troyes* signed by his father.
- In 1429, **Joan of Arc** led a military campaign during which the English forces were pushed back and lost French territory regained.
- In 1437, Henry came of age and began to rule, but his reign was marked by constant turmoil due to his political weaknesses.
- In 1449, hostilities resumed with France, and in 1453, England lost the *Hundred Years' War* and all territory in France except Calais.
- Henry developed a period of mental breakdown during which his cousin, **Richard Duke of York,** became regent and later claimed the throne.

- With Henry's inability to control the feuding nobles, civil war began in 1455 as a result of squabbles between the nobles of England over who should rule, with the crown changing hands several times.
- The conflicts are known as the '*Wars of the Roses*', and although the fighting was very sporadic, there was a general breakdown in the authority and power of the Crown.
- This is a summary of the main stages of the *Wars of the Roses* which was between the **House of York** (white rose) (Fig. 3.32) and the **House of Lancaster** (red rose) (Fig. 3.33):

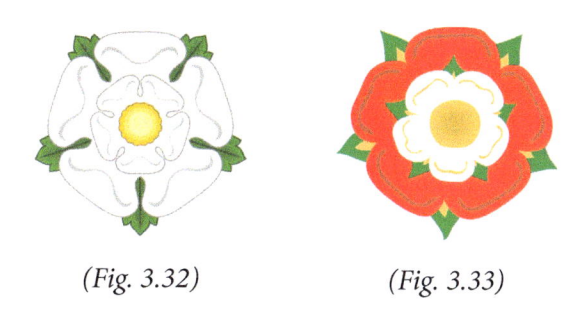

(Fig. 3.32)   *(Fig. 3.33)*

- (**a**) 1455, *First Battle of St. Albans*: Richard Duke of York seized control of the government; (**b**) 1460 *Battle of Northampton*: Richard Neville Earl of Warwick defeated the Lancastrians and took Henry 6th prisoner but Queen Margaret escaped to Scotland; (**c**) 1460, *Battle of Wakefield*: Queen Margaret defeated the Lancastrians and Richard of York was killed; (**d**) 1461, *Battle of Towton*: Earl of Warwick defeated Queen Margaret and Edward 4th is declared king; (**e**) 1464 *Battle of Hexham*: Henry 6th was captured; (**f**) 1469 *Battle of Edgecote*: Warwick defeated Edward 4th; (**g**) 1471, *Battle of Barnet*; Edward defeats Warwick who was killed in battle, Henry 6th was murdered and Edward 4th resumed power and (**h**) 1485, *Battle of Bosworth Field*: Edward's brother Richard 3rd was killed by Lancastrian heir, Henry Tudor, bringing the war to an end.
- This is a summary of who reigned and when: (**a**) **Henry 6th**, Lancastrian, (1422–1461); (**b**) **Edward 4th**, Yorkist (1461–1470); (**c**) **Henry 6th,** Lancastrian restored (1470–1471); and (**d**) **Edward 5th**, Yorkist (April–June 1483).

KING EDWARD 4th

(Fig. 3.34)

- Edward (1442–1483) was *King of England* (1461–1470 and 1471–1483); he was the son of Richard Duke of York and Duchess Cecily; he was also the father of King Edward 5th and the young Richard Duke of York (Princes in the Tower).
- Edward secretly married a widow who was also a commoner, **Elizabeth Woodville** (Fig. 3.35).
- In 1461, **Henry 6th** was deposed by his Yorkist cousin who became **Edward 4th.**

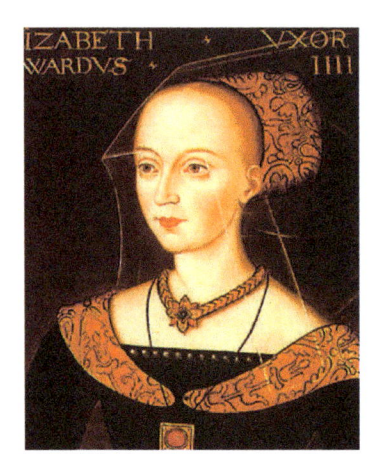

(Fig. 3.35)

House of Plantagenet | 41

- Edward 4th was briefly expelled from the throne in (1470–71) when **Richard Neville** (Earl of Warwick) brought **Henry 6th** back to power.
- Six months later, **Edward 4th** killed Richard Neville in battle (Fig. 3.36) and reclaimed the throne; **Henry 6th** was imprisoned in the Tower of London where he died.

(Fig. 3.36)

- Edward 4th died in 1483, aged only 40 years, and his eldest son and heir **Edward 5th** aged 13 (Fig. 3.37), would have succeeded him, but the king's brother, **Richard Duke of Gloucester** (later King Richard 3rd), declared the king's marriage to be bigamous, making all his children illegitimate.
- **Edward 5th** and his 10-year old brother, **Prince Richard,** were imprisoned in the Tower of London (Fig. 3.38) and possibly murdered by their uncle who became Richard 3rd.

(Fig. 3.37)   (Fig. 3.38)

KING RICHARD 3rd

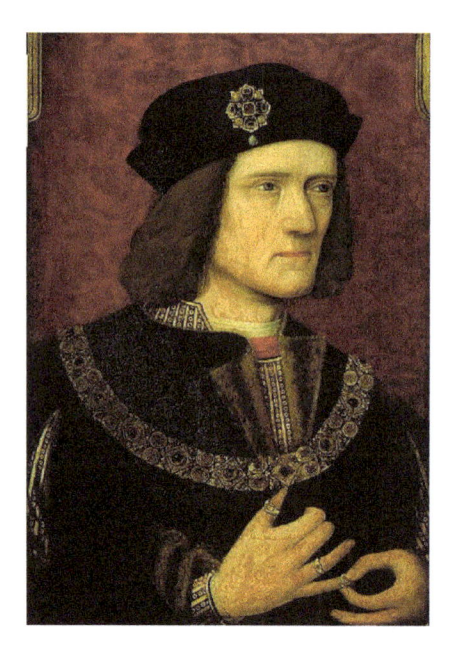

(Fig. 3.39)

- Richard Duke of Gloucester (1452–1485) was *King of England* (1483–1485); he was the son of Richard Plantagenet (Duke of York) and Cecily Neville and the brother of Edward 4th.
- He married **Anne Neville** with whom he had a son.
- Richard was courageous, an excellent administrator, pious, fair, loyal and a devoted husband and father, but he could also be ruthless and vicious.
- **Richard** took the crown by force, and his nephews, **Edward 5th** and **Prince Richard**, were never seen again and presumably died in the Tower; it was widely believed that Richard had them murdered, although their exact fate remains a mystery.
- In 1485, **Henry Tudor**, the last Lancastrian male, landed in England from his exile in France.

- In 1485, **Richard** was defeated and killed aged 32 by **Henry Tudor** at the *Battle at Bosworth Field* (Fig. 3.40) and Henry became **King Henry 7th**.
- Richard 3rd was the last king of the House of York and also last of the Plantagenet Dynasty.

(Fig. 3.40)

4
HOUSE OF TUDOR

46 | History of England

KING HENRY 7th

(Fig. 4.1)

- Henry (1457–1509) was *King of England* (1485–1509) and *Lord of Ireland*; he was the son of Edmund Tudor (Earl of Richmond) and Margaret Beaufort, a descendent of John of Gaunt.
- He married **Elizabeth of York** (Fig. 4.2), daughter of Edward 4th, with whom he had eight children of whom only four survived infancy: **Arthur**, **Margaret**, **Henry** and **Mary**; the marriage united the Houses of York and Lancaster.

(Fig. 4.2)

- In 1485, with Henry's accession to the throne, the *Wars of the Roses* came to an end, and the Tudors continued to rule England for 118 years.
- The nephew of Richard 3rd, **John de la Pole** (Earl of Lincoln), hatched an attempt to claim the throne by using a peasant boy named **Lambert Simnel**, who posed as **Edward** (Earl of Warwick) (the real Warwick was locked up in the Tower of London), to lead an army of German mercenaries supported by Margaret of Burgundy.
- The plotters were defeated and de la Pole was killed at the *Battle of Stoke Field* (1487), and Simnel became an employee in the royal kitchen.
- A more serious imposter was **Perkin Warbeck**, a Flemish youth who posed as **Prince Richard** the son of **Edward 4th** (younger of the two princes in the Tower); again, supported by Margaret of Burgundy, he invaded England four times before he was finally captured and put in the Tower of London, where Warbeck and Edward (Earl of Warwick) were executed.
- Henry formed an understanding with the Spanish **King Ferdinand** and **Queen Isabella** by which their daughter **Catherine** (of Aragon) (Fig. 4.3) would marry his son **Arthur Prince of Wales** (Fig. 4.4).

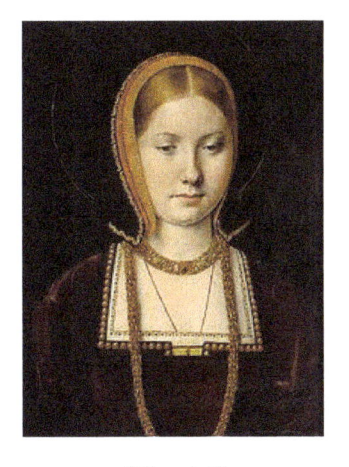

(Fig. 4.3) 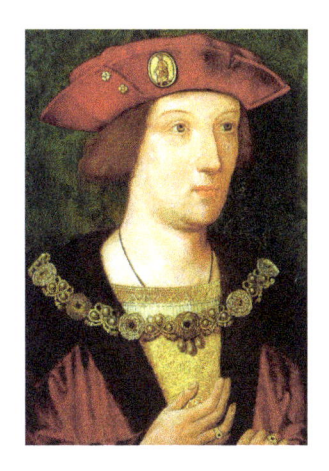   *(Fig. 4.4)*

- Henry formed an alliance with Spain and the **Holy Roman Emperor Maximilian 1st** but in 1493, when they went to war with France, England was dragged into the conflict.
- With his hold on power insecure, Henry reached an understanding with the French and renounced all claims to their territory except the port of Calais.
- In return, the French agreed to recognize him as king and stop sheltering pretenders.
- Henry also reached an understanding with Scotland, agreeing to the marriage of his daughter **Margaret** to **King James 4th of Scotland**.
- In 1501, the King's son, **Arthur**, having married **Catherine of Aragon**, died at the age of 15, leaving his younger son **Henry Duke of York** as heir to the throne.
- In 1509, the King died aged 52 and was succeeded by his son, who became Henry 8th.

KING HENRY 8th

(Fig. 4.5)

- Henry (1491–1547) was *King of England* (1509–1547), and *Lord* and later *King of Ireland*; he was the second son of Henry 7th and Elizabeth of York.
- He married six times (Fig. 4.6), and had three legitimate children who survived infancy: **Mary**, **Elizabeth** and **Edward**.

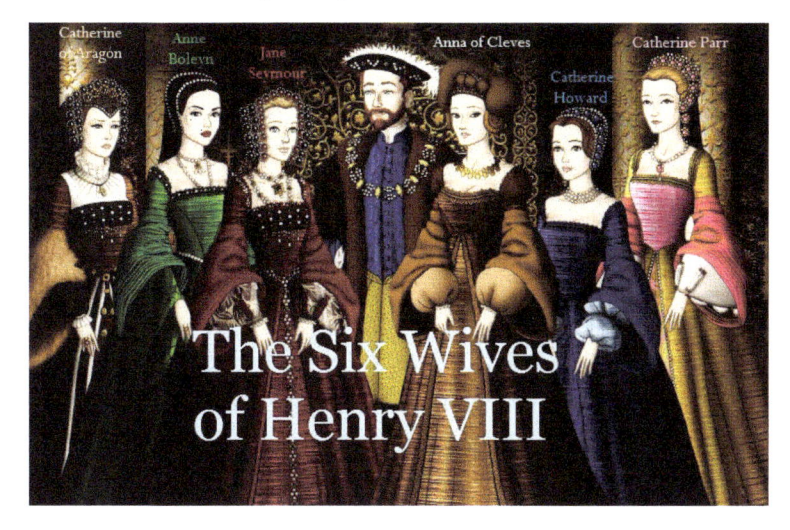

(Fig. 4.6)

- When young, Henry was handsome and athletic in sharp contrast to his wary, miserly father, and he could speak several languages fluently.
- He married his brother's widow, **Catherine of Aragon**, but none of their children survived infancy except a daughter, **Mary** (later Queen Mary Tudor).
- In 1512, the young king embarked on a war with France, despite the fact that his sister Mary was married to **King Louis 12th of France**.
- The war accomplished little and the English Army suffered badly from disease, and Henry was not even present at the one notable victory, the *Battle of the Spurs* (1513).
- Meanwhile, **King James 4th of Scotland** (Fig. 4.7) (despite being Henry's other brother-in-law), activated his alliance with France and declared war on England.
- On September 1513, at the *Battle of Flodden*, the Scots were totally defeated, and King James and most of the Scottish nobility were killed.

(Fig. 4.7)

- In 1520, Henry organised a lavish summit conference in Northern France called the *Field of the Cloth of Gold* during which he met **King Francis 1st of France**.
- **Cardinal Thomas Wolsey** was a very astute politician, of humble background, who became Lord Chancellor and was gifted by Henry with Hampton Court.
- When Catherine was no longer able to have any more children the king became nervous about the possibility of his daughter Mary inheriting the throne.
- Henry decided that he must divorce Catherine and find a new queen.
- The Church would not simply grant this favour, so Henry cited the passage in the Book of Leviticus where it said, "*If a man taketh his brother's wife, he hath committed adultery; they shall be childless.*"
- However, Catherine insisted that her brief marriage to Arthur had not been consummated and that the prohibition did not apply.
- The timing of Henry's case was very unfortunate; it was 1527 and the Pope had been taken prisoner by **Emperor Charles 5th**, Catherine's nephew and the most powerful man in Europe, for siding with his archenemy **King Francis 1st of France**.
- Even Cardinal Wolsey could not persuade the church to grant Henry a divorce; he fell out of favour but died on route to London.

House of Tudor | 51

- As there was no possibility of getting a divorce, Henry decided to secede from the Church, in what became known as the '*English Reformation*'.
- The newly established Church of England was little more than the existing Catholic Church, but with the King rather than the Pope as its head.
- It took a number of years for the separation from Rome to be completed, and many were executed for resisting the king's religious policies including **Sir Thomas More** and **Bishop John Fisher**.
- His marriage to Catherine was declared invalid making Mary illegitimate.
- In 1530, **Queen Catherine** was banished from court and spent the remainder of her life alone in an isolated manor home.
- In 1531, Henry married **Anne Boleyn** in secret, and in September 1533 she gave birth to Elizabeth.
- By now, the king was convinced that his marriage was hexed, and having already found a new queen, **Jane Seymour**, he put Anne Boleyn in the Tower of London on charges of witchcraft; she was accused of adultery and was beheaded along with five men (her brother included).
- That marriage was then declared invalid, so that Elizabeth, just like her half-sister Mary, became a bastard.
- Henry immediately married Jane Seymour, who in October 1537 gave birth to Edward, but the queen died of puerperal sepsis 10 days later.
- In 1540, the king married **Anne of Cleves** for a political alliance with her Protestant brother, the **Duke of Cleves**.
- Anne was a dull, unattractive woman and Henry declined to consummate the marriage; he quickly divorced her, but she remained in England.
- His fifth marriage was to the 19-year-old **Catherine Howard,** but when it became known that she was neither a virgin nor a faithful wife, she ended up on the scaffold and the marriage was declared invalid.
- His sixth and last marriage was to **Catherine Parr**, more a nursemaid to him as his health was failing.
- In 1536, Henry was low on finances and instructed his chief minister **Thomas Cromwell** to close all monasteries.

- This provoked an armed rebellion called the *Pilgrimage of Grace* (1536–37) led by **Robert Aske**, which was ruthlessly put down by the King.
- In 1542, the King embarked on a new campaign against France but only gained the city of Boulogne, which the French re-took within a few years.
- Scotland also declared war and at the *Battle of Solway Moss* (1542) was once again totally defeated by England.
- Henry's paranoia and suspicions worsened in his last years and the number of executions during his 38-year reign numbered tens of thousands.
- In January 1547, the King died at aged 55, and was succeeded by his son, who became Edward 6th.

Cardinal Wolsey

(Fig. 4.8)

- Thomas Wolsey (1473–1530) was a *statesman*, and a *cardinal* of the Roman Catholic Church.
- In 1509, when **King Henry 8th** was crowned, Wolsey became his

almoner, and by 1514, he had become the controlling figure in virtually all matters-of-state.
- In 1515, he was made a cardinal by **Pope Leo 10th** which gave him precedence even over the Archbishop of Canterbury.
- He was then appointed Lord Chancellor and the King's chief adviser, but after failing to negotiate an annulment of Henry's marriage to **Queen Catherine**, Wolsey fell out of favour and retreated to York to fulfil his ecclesiastical duties as Archbishop of York.
- He was recalled to London to answer to charges of treason but died en-route of natural causes.

Thomas Cromwell

(Fig. 4.9)

- Thomas Cromwell (1st Earl of Essex) (1485–1540) was a *lawyer* and *statesman* who served as chief minister to King Henry 8th (1532 –1540.)
- Cromwell, one of the strongest and most powerful advocates of the English Reformation, helped to engineer an annulment of the King's marriage to **Queen Catherine** so that Henry could lawfully marry **Anne Boleyn**.
- In 1534, King Henry failed to obtain the Pope's approval for the annulment so Parliament endorsed the King's claim to be Supreme

Head of the Church of England, giving him the authority to annul his own marriage.
- Cromwell later fell from power after arranging the King's marriage to German princess, **Anne of Cleves.**
- The King found his new bride unattractive and the marriage was annulled six months later.
- In July 1540, Cromwell was executed for treason and heresy; the King later expressed regret at the loss of his chief minister.

Thomas More

(Fig. 4.10)

- Thomas More (1478–1535) was a *lawyer, social philosopher, author* and *statesman;* he was also *Lord High Chancellor of England* (1529–1532).
- In 1516, his book *Utopia,* about the political system of an imaginary ideal island nation, was published.
- More opposed the Protestant Reformation and in particular the theology of **Martin Luthe**r and **William Tyndale**.
- He also opposed the King's separation from the Catholic Church and refused to acknowledge King Henry as the Supreme Head of the Church of England, and the annulment of his marriage to **Catherine of Aragon**.

- After refusing to take the Oath of Supremacy he was convicted of treason and beheaded; his execution, he was reported to have said: "*I die the King's good servant, but God's first.*"
- In 1935, More was canonised by **Pope Pius 11th**.

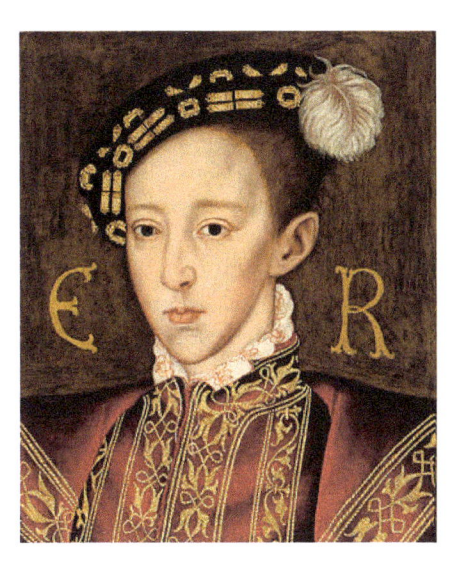

KING EDWARD 6th

(Fig. 4.11)

- Edward (1537–1553) was *King of England* and *Ireland* (1547–1553); he was the son of King Henry 8th and Jane Seymour.
- Edward was pale and frail with a weak constitution, and was only nine years old when he was crowned by **Thomas Cranmer** (Fig. 4.12), the first Protestant Archbishop of Canterbury.
- During Edward's reign, England became a Protestant nation as opposed to a Catholic one in schism from Rome.
- His uncle, **Edward Seymour** (1st Duke of Somerset) (Fig. 4.13), seized power and became Protector, he was popular amongst ordinary people but he tried to curb the power of the barons.

(Fig. 4.12)   (Fig. 4.13)

- In 1549, Somerset and Edward introduced the Book of Common Prayer which was written by Cranmer and contained complete texts for Protestant prayers.
- The book provoked several Catholic rebellions such as *Kett's Rebellion in Norfolk* and the *Prayer Book Rebellion* in Devon and Cornwall.
- In 1550, Somerset was removed from power by **John Dudley** (Earl of Warwick) (Fig. 4.14) who appointed himself Lord President, Duke of Northumberland.

(Fig. 4.14)

House of Tudor | 57

- In 1553, the King died aged 15 of tuberculosis and was succeeded by his half–sister who became Mary 1st Tudor.
- Northumberland made plans to place **Lady Jane Grey** (a sort of grand–niece of Henry 8th) on the throne and marry his son.
- Ninedays later, **Mary,** Edward's half–sister, entered London and had Jane, her husband, and the scheming Northumberland sent to the Tower, where Jane was later beheaded (Fig. 4.15).

(Fig. 4.15)

QUEEN MARY 1st TUDOR

(Fig. 4.16)

- Mary (1516–1558) was *Queen of England* and *Ireland* (1553–1558); she was the daughter of King Henry 8th and Catherine of Aragon.
- Mary married her cousin, **King Philip 2nd of Spain** (Fig. 4.17), but they had no children.
- She was an intelligent and independent-minded woman and a staunch Catholic.
- Mary took the throne amidst popular demonstrations in London, but she never expected to hold the throne, at least not after Edward had been born.
- Being a devoted Catholic, she believed that she could turn the clock back to 1516, before the Reformation began.

(Fig. 4.17)

- Reverting England to Catholicism led to the burnings of 274 Protestants.
- Mary's marriage to Philip 2nd was difficult since she was already in her late 30s and her husband was a foreigner and not welcome in England.
- The union also provoked the hostility of France, who was already at war with Spain, because of the prospect of being completely encircled by the Habsburgs.
- Calais, the last English outpost on the continent, was then taken by France.
- Mary eventually became 'pregnant', or at least believed herself to be, but in reality she may have had uterine cancer.
- In November 1558, the Queen died aged 42, and was succeeded by her half-sister who became Elizabeth 1st.

QUEEN ELIZABETH 1st

(Fig. 4.18)

- Elizabeth (1533–1603) was *Queen of England* and *Ireland* (1558–1603); she was the daughter of King Henry 8th and Ann Boleyn.
- As a child, her guardian and stepfather, Thomas Seymour (husband

of Catherine Parr), behaved improperly towards her and he was later executed.
- As Queen, she restored order to the realm following the turbulence of the reigns of her half-brother, **Edward 6th**, and half-sister, **Mary 1st**.
- The religious issue was partly put to rest by the Elizabethan Religious Settlement, which re-established the Church of England.
- Much of Elizabeth's success was in balancing the interests of the Puritans and Catholics, although she clamped down on Catholics towards the end of her reign.
- In 1570, Elizabeth was excommunicated and **Pope Paul 5th** started to send Catholic missionary priests to England; one of these, a Jesuit, **Edmund Campion**, was tortured and executed, but this strengthened the Catholic cause.
- Elizabeth declined to marry, despite offers from a number of suitors.
- It was rumoured that she was in love with **Robert Dudley** (Earl of Leicester) (Fig. 4.19) whose wife was found dead under suspicious circumstances; Dudley did not marry Elizabeth but was promoted to Lord Protector.
- Her courtiers included **Sir William Cecil** (Lord Burghley) (Fig. 4.20), **Sir Francis Walsingham** (Fig. 4.21), **Robert Devereux** (Earl of Essex) (Fig. 4.22), and **Robert Cecil**.

(Fig. 4.19)

(Fig. 4.20)

(Fig. 4.21)

(Fig. 4.22)

- Elizabeth's government did much to consolidate the work begun under **Thomas Cromwell** in the reign of her father.
- The Queen ran afoul of her cousin, **Mary Queen of Scots**, who was a devoted Catholic and had been forced to abdicate as a consequence (Scotland had recently become Protestant).
- Mary married **King Francis 2nd of France** (Fig. 4.23), and when he died, she married **Henry Stuart** (Lord Darnley) (Fig. 4.24) who murdered Mary's private secretary **David Rizzio**; Darnley was in turn murdered by the **Earl of Bothwell** (Fig. 4.25) who then married Mary.

(Fig. 4.23)   *(Fig. 4.24)*

(Fig. 4.25)

- Mary was deposed and succeeded by her son **King James 6th of Scotland** (later James 1st of England) and fled to England where she was she was immediately arrested and spent the next 18 years in confinement.
- Because Mary was implicated in plots against Elizabeth, she proved to be too dangerous to keep alive, as the Catholic powers in Europe

considered her, not Elizabeth, the legitimate ruler of England; she was eventually tried for treason and beheaded in 1587.
- Elizabeth risked war with Spain by supporting the '*Sea Dogs*' such as **Sir Walter Raleigh** (Fig. 4.26), **Sir John Hawkins** (Fig. 4.27) and **Sir Francis Drake** (Fig. 4.28), who preyed on the Spanish merchant ships carrying gold and silver from the New World.
- In 1588, the Spanish Armada was defeated (Fig. 4.29) by the English fleet commanded by Sir Francis Drake.
- In March 1603, the Queen died aged 69.

(Fig. 4.26)   *(Fig. 4.27)*   *(Fig. 4.28)*

(Fig. 4.29)

5
HOUSE OF STUART

KING JAMES 1st

(Fig. 5.1)

- James (1566–1625) *was King of Scotland* as James 6th (1567–1603) and *King of England* and *Ireland as* James 1st (1603–1625); he was the son of Henry Stuart and Mary Queen of Scots.
- James married **Anne of Denmark** (Fig. 5.2) with whom he had seven children, three of whom survived infancy: **Henry**, **Elizabeth**, and **Charles**.
- He was small, awkward, ungainly but a highly intelligent man; he also had a speech impediment and was given to homosexual tendencies.

(Fig. 5.2)

- James became King of England because he was Queen Elizabeth's closest male Protestant relative; he had already ruled Scotland for more than 30 years before he also became King of England in a Union of the Crowns.
- **King James 1st and 6th**, as he was styled, became the first monarch to rule the entire island of Great Britain, although it was merely a union of the English and Scottish Crowns, and both countries remained separate political entities until 1707.
- James made peace with Spain, and for the first half of the 17th century, England remained largely inactive in European politics.
- James was not a very practical ruler and did not manage Parliament well.
- During his reign two favourite courtiers, **Robert Carr** (Earl of Somerset) (Fig. 5.3) and **George Villiers** (Duke of Buckingham) (Fig. 5.4), became very powerful.
- In 1604, James commissioned the definitive English translation of the Bible.
- He survived several assassination attempts by Catholic conspirators, the Main Plot and Bye Plots of 1603, and the more famous Gunpowder Plot of 5th November 1605, led by **Sir Robert Catesby**; one of the conspirators, **Guy Fawkes** (Fig. 5.5), was found in the cellar with the gunpowder and all were executed.
- In March 1625, the King died aged 58, and was succeeded by his son who became Charles 1st.

(Fig. 5.3) *(Fig. 5.4)*

66 | History of England

(Fig. 5.5)

KING CHARLES 1st

(Fig. 5.6)

- Charles (1600–1649) was *King of England, Scotland* and *Ireland* (1625–1649); he was the son of James 1st of England and Anne of Denmark, and grandson of Mary Queen of Scots.
- Charles married **Henrietta Maria of France** (Fig. 5.6) who was the first cousin of King Louis 14th of France; they had nine children, two of whom became kings (Charles 2nd and James 2nd).
- The Queen was a devout Catholic, which made her unpopular.
- Charles became king only because his elder brother Henry died unexpectedly.

- Charles was influenced by George Villiers (Duke of Buckingham), who was his father's key minister, but Villiers was disliked and alienated Parliament.
- In 1629, Charles dissolved Parliament, not calling another for 11 years during which time he relied on advice from **William Laud** (Archbishop of Canterbury) (Fig. 5.7) and **Thomas Wentworth** (Earl of Strafford) (Fig. 5.8).
- In 1640, Charles recalled Parliament (Long Parliament), which asserted its control over the King, with the impeachment of Laud and execution of Wentworth.

(Fig. 5.7) *(Fig. 5.8)*

- In 1641, the House of Commons reasserted its authority and stipulated that the King should rule in name only; it was strongly Protestant and dominated by independents such as **John Pym** (Fig. 5.9) and **John Eliot.**
- In 1642, Charles entered the Commons with armed men in attendance and tried personally to arrest five of the most extreme MPs for treason, but he was too late and they had escaped.
- Within weeks, the Queen fled to France and the King to Nottingham, where he summoned his subjects to defend his rights on the field of battle.

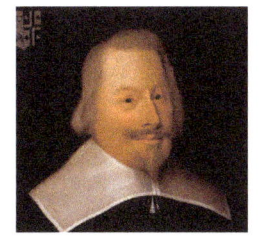

(Fig. 5.9)

Civil Wars

- In 1642, the **First English Civil War** broke out, largely as a result of an ongoing series of conflicts between the King and Parliament.
- The first proper encounter was the *Battle of Edgehill* (1642) in which the Royalists (Cavaliers) led by the King's German nephew, **Prince Rupert of the Rhine** (Fig. 5.10), almost defeated the Parliamentarians (Roundheads) led by the **Earl of Essex** and the **Duke of Manchester**.
- **Oliver Cromwell** then trained a professional cavalry to fight for Parliament, and crushed Prince Rupert's Army at the *Battle of Marston Moor* (1644) (Fig. 5.11).
- In 1645, a newly reorganised 'New Model Army' under Oliver Cromwell and **Sir Thomas Fairfax** (Fig. 5.12) defeated the Royalists at the *Battle of Naseby* (Fig. 5.13), effectively destroying the King's forces.

(Fig. 5.10)

(Fig. 5.11)

(Fig. 5.12)

(Fig. 5.13)

- Charles then deliberately surrendered to the Scottish army, not the English, at Newark, but in early 1647, he was handed over to the English and imprisoned in the Isle of Wight.
- In the **Second English Civil War,** the Scots tried to rescue Charles but were soundly defeated by Cromwell at the *Battle of Preston* (1648).
- The capture and subsequent trial of Charles for treason led to his beheading in January 1649, aged 48, thus making England a republic.

Oliver Cromwell

(Fig. 5.14)

- Oliver Cromwell (1599-1658) was a Puritan and a landowner from Huntingdon, who was an MP for Cambridge.
- He was a superb cavalry commander and trained the New Model Army.
- Having won the Civil War in England, he then scored decisive victories against Royalist armies in Ireland and Scotland.
- In 1653, Cromwell became Lord Protector, making him *'king in all but name'*.
- After he died in 1658, his son, **Richard Cromwell**, succeeded him but proved inadequate and was forced to abdicate within a year.
- For a while it looked as if a new civil war would begin as the New Model Army split into factions, but troops stationed in Scotland under **George Monck** eventually marched on London to restore order.
- In May 1660, Parliament voted to bring back the monarchy.
- There is some debate as to whether Cromwell was a monarch or not.
- Like a king, upon his death the rule was passed on to his son.

KING CHARLES 2nd

(Fig. 5.15)

- Charles (1630–1685) was *King of Scotland* (1649–1651), and *King of England* and *Ireland* (1660–1685); he was the son of King Charles 1st and Henrietta Maria.
- He married **Catherine of Braganza** (Fig. 5.16) but they had no children; the barrenness of the Queen was his lame excuse for his many mistresses, with whom he had at least 15 children.
- Charles was a tall, debonair extrovert who radiated confident promiscuity; he was also a dog-lover and a patron of the arts.

(Fig. 5.16)

- In 1660, the monarchy was restored when **King Charles 2nd** returned to London.
- In 1661, the so-called Cavalier Parliament ordered the bodies of the regicides, including Cromwell, to be disinterred and gruesomely hanged, and those responsible for signing his father's death warrant executed.
- In 1664, a series of naval encounters against the Dutch caused heavy losses on both sides, and the transfer to England of the Dutch colony of New Amsterdam.
- In 1665, London was swept by the *Plague* in which one in five of the population died.
- In 1666, the capital was swept by the *Great Fire* (Fig. 5.17) which destroyed 15,000 buildings.
- In 1667, the Dutch navy brazenly sailed up the Medway to Chatham, where they burnt 13 ships and towed away the navy's flagship, the *Royal Charles*.
- In 1678, a rumour started by a professional liar called **Titus Oates** (Fig. 5.18) claimed that a Popish (Catholic) plot existed to kill the King.

(Fig. 5.17)

(Fig. 5.18)

(Fig. 5.19)

- Although the plot was false, many Catholics were arrested and some put to death, including **Oliver Plunkett** (Archbishop of Armagh) (Fig. 5.19).
- During Charles' reign, two political parties developed, the Tories who believed that the King's right to rule was sanctioned by God (they were impeccable supporters of the Church of England), and the Whigs who had a more down-to-earth view of the King's power.
- In 1685, following a stroke, the King converted to Catholicism on his deathbed, and died aged 54, to be succeeded by his brother who became James 2nd.

KING JAMES 2nd

(Fig. 5.20)

- James (1633–1701) was *King of England* and *Ireland* as James 2nd, and *King of Scotland* as James 7th (1685–1668); he was the son of King Charles 1st and Henrietta Maria, and the brother of King Charles 2nd.
- James was a staunch Catholic but was tolerant of other religions and was the last Catholic monarch of the three kingdoms.
- He came to power after a distinguished military career but had a brittle and humourless personality.
- His magnificent coronation was attended by **Henry Purcell** and **Samuel Pepys**.
- James married twice, firstly to **Anne Hyde** (Fig. 5.21) with whom he had several children, but only two daughters survived: **Mary** (who married **William of Orange**) and **Anne** (who became **Queen Anne**).
- When Anne Hyde died, he married Italian **Princess Mary of Modena** who in 1688 gave birth to **James Francis Edward Stuart** (later the 'Old Pretender') (Fig. 5.22).
- Because the new heir was a Catholic, several influential Protestants claimed that the child was '*suppositious*' and had been brought to the Queen's bedchamber in a warming pan.

House of Stuart | 75

(Fig. 5.21)   (Fig. 5.22)

- **James Francis Edward Stuart** (Fig. 5.23) later married **Maria Klementina Sobieska**, granddaughter of **King John 3rd Sobieski** of Poland; one of their sons was **Charles Edward Stuart** (Bonnie Prince Charlie – later the 'Young Pretender') (Fig. 5.24).
- In 1685, King James suppressed a rebellion by a pretender, the Protestant **Duke of Monmouth** (Fig. 5.25), the oldest illegitimate son of his brother Charles 2nd.
- Monmouth was routed at the *Battle of Sedgemoor* (1685) and he and his rebels were tried by **Judge Jeffreys** and executed.

(Fig. 5.23)

(Fig. 5.24)   (Fig. 5.25)

- Second-in-command of the King's forces, fighting against Monmouth, was the young **John Churchill.**
- In June 1688, in order to prevent a Catholic succession, several Protestant officers (Immortal Seven) requested military intervention by the Protestant Dutch **Stadholder William 3rd of Orange** (James' son-in-law who had married his daughter Mary).
- William was not king of the Netherlands but a Stadholder, leader of the Dutch provinces and head of the army.
- In November 1688, William landed in England with an invading force, and although James had the larger army, he was not prepared to fight and lost all authority.
- Many Protestant officers including John Churchill, and the King's daughter, Anne, deserted and joined William, and James was allowed to escape to France.
- James lived in France, a broken man, until his death in 1701 aged 68.

KING WILLIAM 3rd AND QUEEN MARY 2nd

(Fig. 5.26)

- William of Orange (1650–1702) was *King of England, Scotland* and *Ireland* and *Prince of Orange* (1689–1702); he was the son of William 2nd of Orange and Mary, daughter of Charles 1st.
- Mary (1662–1694) was joint sovereign of *England, Scotland* and *Ireland* (1689–1694); she was the daughter of King James 2nd.
- Mary was a likeable person, who loved her husband and her people, but William was not popular preferring the company of his Dutch courtiers.

- In 1689 **Mary** and her husband, **William 3rd of Orange**, were jointly enthroned in what became known as the *Glorious Revolution*; although they ruled as joint monarchs, the real power rested with the King.
- In December 1689, the *Bill of Rights* confirmed many provisions of the earlier Declaration of Right that established restrictions on the royal prerogative; it also stated that '*no Catholic can become king or queen*'.
- William was opposed to the imposition of such constraints, but he chose not to engage in a conflict with Parliament and agreed to abide by the statute.
- In 1690, **King James 2nd** attempted to retake the throne by force but was decisively defeated by **King William 3rd** at the *Battle of the Boyne* in Ireland (Fig. 5.27).

(Fig. 5.27)

- After the war, Catholics were made second–class citizen under the thumb of the Protestants who dominated Parliament; ever since, Irish Catholics have decried the *Battle of the Boyne* while militant Protestants have celebrated it.
- In 1694, the Queen died of smallpox, aged 32, and William ruled alone for the next eight years.
- William fought a long, expensive and unpopular war with **Louis 14th of France**.
- He appointed **John Churchill** (1st Duke of Marlborough) to command a grand coalition of English, Dutch and Austrian forces against the French.
- In 1702, William 3rd died aged 51, following a riding accident that resulted in pneumonia.

Jacobite Uprisings

- In parts of Scotland and Ireland, Catholics loyal to **King James 2nd** remained determined to see him restored to the throne, and there followed a series of bloody though unsuccessful uprisings.
- As a result of these, any failure to pledge loyalty to the victorious King William was severely dealt with; the most infamous example of this policy was the *Massacre of Glencoe* (1692).
- Jacobite rebellions continued into the mid–18th century until the son of James 2nd and the last Catholic claimant to the throne **James Francis Edward Stuart** ('Old Pretender'), mounted a final campaign in 1745.
- In 1746, the Jacobite forces of **Prince Charles Edward Stuart** (Bonnie Prince Charlie – Young Pretender) were defeated at the *Battle of Culloden*.

QUEEN ANNE

(Fig. 5.28)

- Anne (1665–1714) was *Queen of Great Britain* and *Ireland* (1702–1714); she was the younger daughter of King James 2nd and Anne Hyde.
- In 1702, Anne inherited the throne because she was a Protestant and because William and Mary died childless; she was the last monarch of the House of Stuart.
- She married **Prince George**, son of the King of Denmark, with whom she had 18 pregnancies that led to a series of miscarriages and stillbirths; two children lived for a few months, and one lived to be eleven.
- Anne was popular but unattractive and obese.
- In 1713, the *Treaty of Utrecht* was signed between France and England.
- In 1714, the Queen died aged 49, and was succeeded by her German cousin who became George 1st.

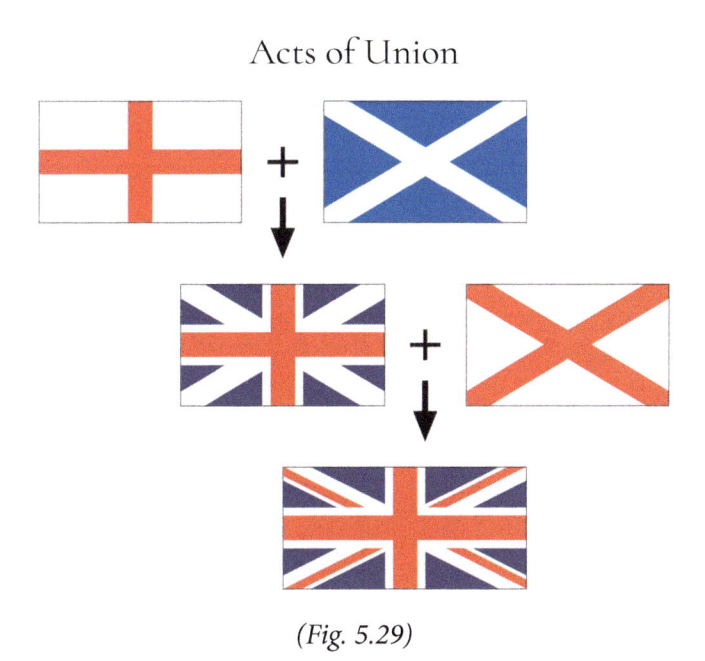

Acts of Union

(Fig. 5.29)

- In 1707, the Acts of Union between the Kingdom of England and the Kingdom of Scotland dissolved both Parliaments and formed a **Kingdom of Great Britain** governed by a unified Parliament of Great Britain.

- The Acts joined the two Kingdoms (previously separate states, with separate legislatures but with the same monarch) into a single Kingdom of Great Britain.
- The two countries had shared a monarch since the Union of the Crowns in 1603, when King James 6th of Scotland inherited the English Throne from his distant cousin Queen Elizabeth 1st.
- Although described as a Union of Crowns, until 1707, there were in fact two separate crowns resting on the same head.
- The Acts took effect on 1st May 1707, when the Scots Parliament and the English Parliament united to form the Parliament of Great Britain based in the Palace of Westminster in London, the home of the English Parliament; hence the Acts are referred to as the **Union of the Parliaments**.
- The Act of Union of 1800 formally assimilated **Ireland** within the British political process and from 1st January 1801 created a new state called the **United Kingdom of Great Britain and Ireland**, which united the Kingdom of Great Britain with the Kingdom of Ireland to form a single political entity.
- The English capital of London was adopted as the capital of the Union.

6
HOUSE OF HANOVER

KING GEORGE 1st

(Fig. 6.1)

- George Louis (1660–1727) was *King of Great Britain* and *Ireland*, and *Elector of Hanover* (1714–1727); he was the son of Ernst August, Duke of Brunswick-Luneburg and Elector-designate of Hanover, and Sophia of Palatine.
- George married and later divorced **Princess Sophia Dorothea of Celle;** they had two children (Fig. 6.2).
- George became king at the age of 54; the oldest monarch in history.
- He was short, overweight, bad-tempered, and lacked manners and charm.
- George remained essentially German; although he spoke several languages, his English was rudimentary and he spent a lot of time in Hanover.
- His descendants, however, became more and more British, and presided over a time during which Britain's power in the world grew dramatically.

(Fig. 6.2)

- **Handel** worked for George and the '*Water Music*' was composed for a royal occasion.
- In 1715, just a year after his coronation, the first Jacobite rebellion under **James Francis Edward Stuart** started in *Braemar* but was crushed with ease.
- Because George spoke little English, his son **George Augustus** came to cabinet meetings to translate, but the young Prince of Wales, soon fell out with his father.
- In 1720, the King fell victim to a scam called the *'South Sea Bubble'* and lost a lot of money but was tarred with the same brush as the criminals.
- The King favoured the Whigs, and in 1721, **Robert Walpole** became the first Prime Minister of Britain, a post he kept permanently for the next 20 years.
- In 1727, on one of his visits to Hanover, the King had a stroke and died, aged 67, and was succeeded by his son who became George 2nd.

KING GEORGE 2nd

(Fig. 6.3)

- George Augustus (1683–1760) was *King of Great Britain* and *Ireland* and *Elector of Hanover* (1727–1760); he was the son of King George 1st and Sophia Dorothea.
- George married **Caroline of Brandenburg-Ansbach** (Fig. 6.4) with whom he had eight children.

(Fig. 6.4)

- He came to the throne when he was 43, and reigned for 33 years; his coronation was magnificent with music by **Handel**.
- He was the last British monarch to be born outside Great Britain; he spoke English well but with a German accent.
- George was more interested in politics than his father and was more popular.
- Although George was a pompous man of little intelligence, he was helped by an able Prime Minister, **Robert Walpole**, and an intelligent consort, **Queen Caroline**.
- George was very courageous in battle, and when in his twenties, he fought under the **Duke of Marlborough** at the *Battle of Oudenarde* (1708).
- George was involved in Jacobite rebellions: in September 1745, the **Young Pretender** defeated the royal army at the *Battle of Prestonpans*; and in April 1746, the Jacobites were defeated at the *Battle of Culloden*.
- George became involved in a series of wars, most notably: *War of Captain Jenkin's Ear* (1739), *War of Austrian Succession* (1740–1748) and *Seven Years War* (1756–1763).
- In 1743, at the *Battle of Dettingen* (Fig. 6.5), during the *War of Austrian Succession*, George was the last British monarch to personally lead troops into battle.

(Fig. 6.5)

- George's eldest son, **Frederick, Prince of Wales** did not get on with his parents, who sidelined him in favour of his younger brother, William Augustus.
- Because of this, the Prince of Wales became a focus for those that opposed his father and Walpole.
- Although Prince Frederick hoped to be king, he died suddenly in 1751 aged 44, while George was still alive; and Frederick's son, **George William Frederick**, became **King George 3rd**.
- During the latter years of George's reign, the British were winning the struggle for empire against the French.
- In 1760, the King died aged 76 from a heart attack and was succeeded by his grandson, who became George 3rd.

KING GEORGE 3rd

(Fig. 6.6)

- George William Frederick (1738–1820) was *King of Great Britain* and *Ireland* (1760–1801), *Elector of Hanover* (1720–1820) and *King of the United Kingdom of Great Britain* and *Ireland* (1801–1820); he was the son of Frederick, Prince of Wales and Augusta of Saxe-Coburg, and the grandson of George 2nd.
- He married **Charlotte of Mecklenburg-Strelitz** (Fig. 6.7), and they had 15 children.

(Fig. 6.7)

- George succeeded his father as Prince of Wales when he was 12, and became King at the age of 22.
- He was the first Hanovarian king to be born in England with English as his mother tongue; he was proud to be British born and bred, took no interest in Hanover and never went there.
- George was well-built, cheerful and good-natured; he ate and drank in moderation, and disapproved of gambling; he was also very devout and spent hours praying.
- The first 10 years of his reign saw Prime Ministers come and go, notably: **John Stuart** (Earl of Bute), **Charles Watson-Wentworth** (Marquis of Rockingham), **William Pitt** (Earl of Chatham) and **Frederick North** (Lord North).
- George is remembered as the ruler who lost the North American Colonies, and who saw the rise to independence of the United States of America.
- Despite this, his reign saw gain in other overseas territories that formed the basis of Britain's 19th century Empire.
- In 1800, the King survived an attempted assassination by **James Hadfield**.
- In 1788, at the age of 50, the King showed signs of mental derangement which subsequently abated.

- In 1804, the illness recurred and by 1810 the King became very ill and demented, probably as a result of acute intermittent porphyria.
- In 1811, he was declared unfit to rule and his son acted as regent.
- George spent the last years of his life completely blind and wandering around a deserted Windsor Castle.
- He is remembered as a rather pathetic figure in his madness; as a sane man, he is remembered as an incompetent king who provoked a war that brought about the loss of American colonies.
- In January 1820, the King died of pneumonia, aged 81, and was succeeded by two of his sons, who became George 4th and William 4th, both of whom died without legitimate children.
- Important events during King George 3rd's reign include; the French revolution (1789); Nelson's victory at the *Battle of the Nile* (1798) Nelson's victory at the *Battle of Trafalgar* (1805); and Wellington's victory at *Battle of Waterloo* (1815).

Industrial Revolution

- The Industrial Revolution was the transition to new manufacturing processes in the period from about 1760 to about 1840.
- The Revolution began in Great Britain and most of the important technological innovations were British.
- This transition included going from hand production methods to machines, and the textile industry was the first to use modern production methods.
- The Industrial Revolution marks a major turning point in history.
- At approximately the same time the Industrial Revolution was occurring, Britain was undergoing an agricultural revolution which also helped to improve living standards and provided surplus labour available for industry.
- The First Industrial Revolution evolved into the Second Industrial Revolution in the transition years between 1840 and 1870, when technological and economic progress continued with the increasing adoption of steam transport and the large-scale manufacture of machine tools and the increasing use of machinery in steam-powered factories.

KING GEORGE 4th

(Fig. 6.8)

- George Augustus Frederick was *King of the United Kingdom of Great Britain* and *Ireland*, and the *Elector of Hanover* (1820–1830); he was the son of King George 3rd and Charlotte of Mecklenburg–Strelitz.
- George married **Caroline of Brunswick–Wolfenbuttel** (Fig. 6.9) with whom he had one daughter.
- He spent 10 years as Prince Regent (1811–1821), when his father was indisposed, supposedly governing the country, but in reality he was spending money on himself.
- In January 1820, he acceded to the throne aged 58 and had a lavish coronation attended by **Sir Walter Scott**.
- George was one of Britain's least popular monarchs, he and his dandy friends like **George 'Beau' Brummell** (Fig. 6.10) spent a fortune gorging and drinking.
- Following the death of **Queen Caroline** in 1821, he married a Catholic widow, **Mrs. Maria FitzHerbert** (Fig. 6.11), in secret and then lied about doing so.
- Perhaps his greatest achievement was artistic patronage, and the creation of Regent's Park and the Royal Pavilion in Brighton (Fig. 6.12).
- In June 1830, the King died unlamented aged 67 and was succeeded by his brother who became William 4th.

(Fig. 6.9)

(Fig. 6.10)  (Fig. 6.11)

(Fig. 6.12)

KING WILLIAM 4th

(Fig. 6.13)

- William Henry (1765–1837) was *King of the United Kingdom of Great Britain* and *Ireland* and *Elector of Hanover* (1830–1837); he was the third son of King George 3rd and Charlotte Mecklenburg-Strelitz and the brother of King George 4th.
- William married **Adelaide of Saxe-Meiningen** (Fig. 6.14) and had two daughters who died young.
- He was the oldest person to ever accede to the British throne at the age of 64, and was more popular than his brother George 4th.
- In contrast to his predecessor, he was frugal and had a low-key coronation.
- He disliked ceremony and fuss, spoke his mind, and detested foreigners, especially the French; he took no interest in art, literature or science.
- He spent the early years of his life in the navy, and became a friend of **Horatio Nelson**, and is sometimes called '*Sailor Bill*'.
- In 1785, William was made a Rear Admiral and Duke of Clarence, and in 1811 he became an Admiral of the Fleet.
- William lived in Clarence House and liked to walk the street unguarded.

(Fig. 6.14)

- Between 1790 and 1811 he lived with his mistress, an actress called **Mrs. Jordan**, who bore him 10 children.
- In 1831, he encouraged the passage of the first *Reform Act*, which marked Britain's progress towards full democracy; the Tory–dominated House of Lords was attempting to block the bill, but the King created sufficient Whig peers to pass the bill and for the act to become law.
- He was very fond of his young niece, **Princess Victoria** (Fig. 6.15).
- In 1834, a great fire destroyed Westminster Palace.
- In 1837, the King died aged 71, and was succeeded by his niece who became Queen Victoria.

(Fig. 6.15)

QUEEN VICTORIA

(Fig. 6.16)

- Alexandrina Victoria (1819–1901) was *Queen of the United Kingdom of Great Britain* and *Ireland* (1837–1901) and *Empress of India* (1877–1901); she was the daughter of Edward Augustus, Duke of Kent (Fig. 6.17), the fourth son of King George 3rd and Princess Victoria of Saxe–Coburg–Saalfeld (Fig. 6.18).

(Fig. 6.17)    *(Fig. 6.18)*

- Victoria was short and not beautiful; she spoke German, French and Italian, she was warm-hearted, quick-tempered, vivacious and emotional.
- When the 18-year-old Princess came to the throne in June 1837, the reputation of the monarchy had been considerably damaged by the four Georges and only partially restored by **King William 4th**, her uncle.
- At the time of her accession, the government was led by the Whig Prime Minister **Lord Melbourne,** who Victoria liked and relied on for advice, and was very distressed when he had to resign in 1839.
- She did not at first like the Tory Prime Minister, **Sir Robert Peel,** but under her husband's influence she came to admire him.
- In 1840, she married her first cousin, a German Prince, **Albert Augustus Charles Emmanuel of Saxe-Coburg and Gotha** with whom she had nine children (Fig. 6.19), all of whom survived to adulthood; their marriage was strong and loving.
- Many of her children married into European royal families; her granddaughters included the Queens of Sweden, Norway, Greece, Romania and Spain, and the Tsarina of Russia; her grandson became **Kaiser William 2nd of Germany**.
- In the 1840s, the Queen survived several assassination attempts.

(Fig. 6.19)

House of Hanover | 95

- In 1851, the Queen and Prince Albert opened the Great Exhibition at Crystal Palace, which attracted millions of visitors from around the world.
- In 1861, Prince Albert died unexpectedly at the age of 42, and the Queen plunged into deep morning and withdrew from public life.
- In 1867, **Benjamin Disraeli** became Prime Minister and encouraged the Queen back to public life.
- Disraeli was replaced by the Liberal, **William Gladstone**, who was much less popular.
- In 1874, Disraeli was returned to power at the general election.
- In 1877, Victoria became Empress of India.
- In September 1896, the Queen became the longest-reigning monarch (Fig. 6.20), when she surpassed the previous record, set by George 3rd, of 59 years and 96 days.
- In 1897, Victoria celebrated the 60th anniversary of her accession to the throne.
- In 1900, her health began to decline and she spent her final weeks at Osborne House where she died of a stroke, aged 82.
- When Victoria died, after a reign of 63 years, the monarchy was once again a well-respected and essential British institution, and the Empire spanned 20% of global territory.
- Her death also marked the end of the '*Victorian Age*'; Victoria was the last monarch of the House of Hanover, and her son and successor, Edward 7th, belonged to the house of Saxe-Coburg and Gotha.

(Fig. 6.20)

7
HOUSE OF SAXE-COBURG AND GOTHA

KING EDWARD 7th

(Fig. 7.1)

- Albert Edward was *King of the United Kingdom of Great Britain* and *Ireland* and *Emperor of India* (1901–1910); he was the eldest son of Queen Victoria and Prince Albert; he was known as '*Bertie*' to his family throughout his life.
- As a child, he was not a distinguished student but he was charming and sociable.
- Because of his mother's long reign, Edward spent a large part of his life as Prince of Wales.
- Edward married **Princess Alexandra of Denmark** (Fig. 7.2), with whom he had seven children.

(Fig. 7.2)

- He had many mistresses throughout his married life, notably: **Lillie Langtry**, **Alice Keppel**, **Lady Randolph Churchill**, **Countess of Warwick**, and **Lady Vane-Tempest**.
- As Prince of Wales, William enjoyed cordial relations with **William Gladstone** and he was a patron of the arts and sciences and opened the Royal College of Music in 1883.
- He enjoyed gambling and country sports and was a keen hunter; he also took a keen interest in horseracing.
- In 1901, he ascended to the throne at the age of 59 (Figs 7.3 and 7.4), but his coronation was delayed because he developed acute appendicitis, which was successfully treated by **Sir Frederick Treves** (Fig. 7.5) supported by **Lord Lister** (Fig. 7.6).
- Edward was known as the '*Uncle of Europe*' because he was related to nearly every other European monarch, for example, **Kaiser William 2nd** (Fig. 7.7) was his nephew, **Tsar Nicholas 2nd** was his nephew by marriage, **Tsarina Alexandra** of Russia was his niece, **King Frederick 7th of Denmark** was his brother-in-law, and **King Albert 1st of Belgium** was his second cousin.

(Fig. 7.3)

(Fig. 7.4)

(Fig. 7.5)

(Fig. 7.6)

- As king, his main interests were foreign affairs and naval and military matters, and he encouraged the modernization of the Home Fleet and Army after the Second Boer War.
- Fluent in French and German, he made a number of visits abroad, and fostered good relations with France, but his relationship with his nephew Kaiser William 2nd was poor.
- Towards the end of his life, the King increasingly suffered from bronchitis.
- In May 1910, the King died of a heart attack aged 69 and was succeeded by his son who became George 5th.

(Fig. 7.7)

8
HOUSE OF WINDSOR

First World War

- The First World War (WW1) originated in Europe and lasted from 28th July, 1914 to 11th November, 1918.
- More than 70 million military personnel were mobilised in one of the largest wars in history.
- The two opposing alliances were: the *Allies* (Russia, France and the United Kingdom of Great Britain and Ireland) versus the *Central Powers* (Germany and Austria–Hungary).
- The trigger for the war was the assassination of **Archduke Franz Ferdinand** (Fig. 8.1), heir to the throne of Austria–Hungary, in Sarajevo on 28th June 1914.

(Fig. 8.1)

- On 28th July, Austria–Hungary declared war on Serbia, and Russia mobilised in support of Serbia.
- Germany then invaded neutral Belgium and Luxemburg before moving towards France, and the United Kingdom declared war on Germany.
- The German march on Paris was halted, and the Western Front settled into a battle of attrition with a trench line (Fig. 8.2) that changed little until 1917.
- On the Eastern Front, the Russian army was successful against the Austro–Hungarians, but the Germans stopped its invasion of East Prussia.

(Fig. 8.2)

- In November 1914, the Ottoman Empire joined the Central Powers, and in 1915, Italy joined the Allies and Bulgaria joined the Central Powers; Romania joined the Allies in 1916 as did the United States in 1917.
- The Russian government collapsed in March 1917 and a revolution in November followed by a further military defeat brought the Russians (Fig. 8.3) to terms with the Central Powers via the *Treaty of Brest Litovsk* which granted the Germans a significant victory.
- In the spring of 1918, the Allies drove back the Germans in a series of successful offences.
- On 4th November, 1918, Austria–Hungary and a week later Germany agreed to an armistice ending the war in victory for the Allies; the four empires (German, Austro–Hungarian, Russian and Ottoman) ceased to exist.

(Fig. 8.3)

- National borders were redrawn, with several independent nations restored or created, and Germany's colonies were confiscated.
- In 1919, during the *Paris Peace Conference* the big four (Britain, France, the United States and Italy) imposed their terms in a series of treaties.
- The League of Nations was formed with the aim of preventing any repetition of such a conflict, but this failed and economic depression, renewed nationalism, weakened successor states, and feelings of humiliation (particularly in Germany) eventually contributed to WW2.

KING GEORGE 5th

(Fig. 8.4)

- George Frederick Ernest Albert (1865-1936) was the *King of the United Kingdom of Great Britain* and *Ireland* and *Emperor of India* (1910–1936); he was the second son of King Edward 7th and Queen Alexandra; he was also the first cousin of Tsar Nicholas 2nd and Kaiser William 2nd.

- George married his late brother's fiancée, **Princess Mary of Teck** (Fig. 8.5), with whom he had six children: **Edward** (later Edward 8th and Duke of Windsor); **Albert** (later George 6th); **Mary** (later Princess Royal and Countess of Harewood); **Henry, George** and **John**.
- In 1892, George became heir to his father, then Prince of Wales, on the death of his elder brother **Albert Duke of Clarence** (Fig. 8.6), at the age of 28.
- King George became the first member of the *House of Windsor* which he renamed from the *House of Saxe-Coburg and Gotha* as a result of anti-German public sentiment.
- In January 1936, the King died aged 70 and was succeeded by his eldest son who became Edward 8th.

(Fig. 8.5)   *(Fig. 8.6)*

KING EDWARD 8th

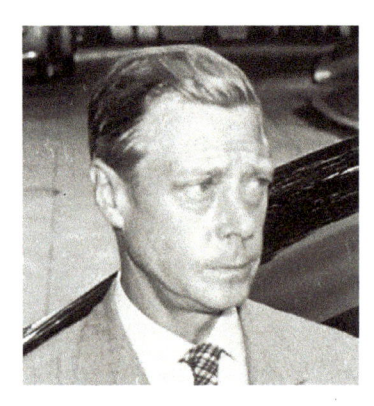

(Fig. 8.7)

- Edward Albert Christian (1894–1972) was *King of the United Kingdom of Great Britain* and *Ireland*, and *Emperor of India* (from January–December 1936); he was the eldest son of George Duke of York (later King George 5th) and Mary Duchess of York (later Queen Mary), and was known as 'David'.
- When Edward was born, Queen Victoria was still alive and there were three direct heirs to the throne; her *son* (later King Edward 7th), her grandson (later King George 6th) and her great-grandson (later King Edward 8th).
- In July 1911, he was officially invested as the Prince of Wales (Fig. 8.8), at Caernarvon Castle.

(Fig. 8.8)

- During WW1, the prince had a commission with the Grenadier Guards.
- Edward enjoyed fashionable society and pursued married women who were usually older than him; such as **Freda Dudley Ward** and **Thelma Lady Furness**.
- In 1934, Edward met and fell in love with an American, **Mrs. Wallis Simpson** (Fig. 8.9), who at the time was married to **Ernest Simpson**, having divorced her first husband.

(Fig. 8.9)

- In January 1936, he became King, and in December of that year, when informed by Prime Minister **Stanley Baldwin** that marriage to Wallis was unacceptable, he abdicated and was created **Duke of Windsor**.
- In June 1937, the ex-king married Wallis Simpson in France.
- In 1938, the Duke and Duchess visited Germany where they met **Adolf Hitler,** and were accused of having pro–Nazi sympathies.
- During the war, he served as Governor of the Bahamas and spent the rest of his life in retirement (Fig. 8.10) in Paris, where he died in 1972, aged 77.

(Fig. 8.10)

KING GEORGE 6th

(Fig. 8.11)

- Albert Frederick Arthur George (1895–1952) was *King of the United Kingdom of Great Britain* and the *Dominions of the Commonwealth* (1936–1952) and *Emperor of India* (1936–1947); he was the last Emperor of India and the first Head of the Commonwealth, and was the second son of George Duke of York (later King George 5th) and Mary Duchess of York (later Queen Mary), and never expected nor wished to succeed to the throne.
- In 1923, he married **Lady Elizabeth Bowes–Lyon** (Fig. 8.12) with whom he had two daughters, **Elizabeth** and **Margaret**.
- He fought as a young naval officer in Jutland in WW1 and was the first member of the Royal Family to learn to fly.
- In December 1936, he became **King George 6th** following the abdication of his brother, **King Edward 8th**, and was crowned on 12th May 1937 (Fig. 8. 13).
- During WW2, the royal couple stayed in London despite German bombing raids.
- In the later years of his reign, the King was beset by health problems, including arteriosclerosis, possibly Buerger's disease and lung cancer,

(Fig. 8.12)

(Fig. 8.13)

no doubt precipitated by his heavy smoking, and in September 1951, his left lung was removed.
- In February 1952, the King died during his sleep aged 56.
- His daughter flew back to Britain from a visit to Kenya as Queen Elizabeth 2nd.

Second World War

- The Second World War (WW2) lasted from 1939 to 1945.
- The war began on 1st September 1939 with the invasion of Poland by Germany (Fig. 8.14) and subsequent declarations of war on Germany by France and the United Kingdom.

(Fig. 8.14)

- From late 1939 to early 1941, Germany conquered or controlled much of continental Europe, and formed the Axis alliance with Italy and Japan.
- Under the *Molotov–Ribbentrop Pact* of August 1939, Germany and the Soviet Union annexed territories of their European neighbours (Poland, Finland, Romania, and the Baltic States).
- In June 1941, the European Axis powers launched an invasion of the Soviet Union.
- In December 1941, Japan attacked the United States and European colonies and quickly conquered much of the Western Pacific.
- The Axis advance was halted in 1942 when Japan lost the critical *Battle of Midway*, and Germany was defeated in North Africa and Stalingrad.

- In 1943, the Allies invaded Sicily, and the subsequent invasion of Italy brought about Italian surrender. With the allied victories in the Pacific, the Axis lost the initiative and undertook strategic retreat on all fronts.
- In 1944, the Western Allies invaded German-occupied France while the Soviet Union regained all its territorial losses and invaded Germany and its allies.
- The war in Europe was concluded with an invasion of Germany that culminated in the capture of Berlin by Soviet troops and the subsequent German unconditional surrender on 8th May 1945.
- The refusal of Japan to surrender resulted in the dropping of atomic bombs on the cities of Hiroshima (6th August) and Nagasaki (9th August) and the end of the war in Asia.

QUEEN ELIZABETH 2nd

(Fig. 8.15)

(Fig. 8.16)

- Elizabeth Alexandra Mary (b. 1926) is *Queen of the United Kingdom of Great Britain* and *Northern Ireland*; she is the daughter of Albert Duke of York (later King George 6th) and Elizabeth Duchess of York (later Queen Elizabeth).
- In 1947, she married **Prince Philip Mountbatten of Greece** (Fig. 8.16) (later Duke of Edinburgh).
- They have four children: **Charles** (Prince of Wales) (1948), **Anne** (Princess Royal) (1950), **Andrew** (Duke of York) (1960), and **Edward** (Earl of Wessex) (1964).
- Elizabeth became Queen on 6th February 1952, and her reign has seen the Commonwealth take the place of the British Empire.
- The Queen makes an official visit to a Commonwealth country every year and receives reciprocal visits.
- In December 1957, Elizabeth made the first of her televised Christmas broadcasts.
- In 1977, she celebrated 25 years of her reign (Silver Jubilee); in 2002, 50 years (Golden Jubilee); and in 2012, 60 years (Diamond Jubilee).
- 1992 was the Queen's '*Annus Horribilis*' because it marked the separation of **Prince Andrew** from his wife, the divorce of **Princess Anne,** the separation of **Prince Charles** from his wife as well as the fire at Windsor Castle.

- 1997 saw the tragic death of **Princess Diana** and in 2002 the Queen lost her mother **Queen Elizabeth** and sister **Princess Margaret** (Fig. 8.17).
- In 2005, her son Prince Charles married **Camilla Parker-Bowles** (Fig. 8.18), and in 2011 her grandson **Prince William** married **Kate Middleton** (Fig. 8.19); her great-grandson, **George** was born in 2013 and her great-granddaughter **Charlotte** in 2015 and her great-grandson **Louis** in 2018.

(Fig. 8.17)

(Fig. 8.18)

(Fig. 8.19)

9
POLITICIANS

ROBERT WALPOLE, 1st EARL OF ORFORD

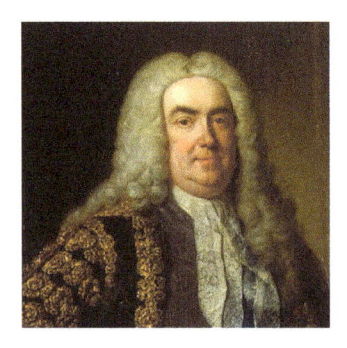

(Fig. 9.1)

- Sir Robert Walpole (1676–1745) was Prime minister (PM) during the reigns of George 1st and George 2nd; he is regarded as being the first PM in the modern age and the longest serving.
- In 1702, he first entered the Commons as a Whig Member of Parliament (MP) for *Castle Ridge*.
- He was PM in 1721–1742 and was succeeded by **Spencer Compton, 1st Earl of Wilmington** (Fig. 9.2).
- During his tenure, Walpole played a significant role in sustaining the Whig party, safeguarding the Hanoverian succession, and defending the principles of the Glorious Revolution.
- He resigned after a vote of no confidence after failing to deal with the *War of Jenkins' Ear*.
- He died in 1745, aged 68.

(Fig. 9.2)

THOMAS PELHAM–HOLLES, 1st DUKE OF NEWCASTLE

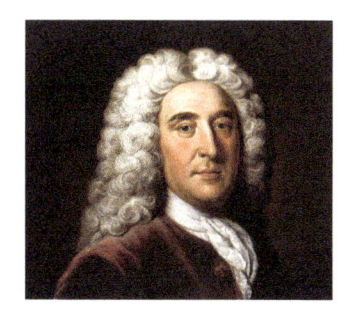

(Fig. 9.3)

- Thomas Pelham–Holles (1693–1768) was a Whig protégé of Sir Robert Walpole.
- After his brother, **Henry Pelham's** (Fig. 9.4) death, Newcastle twice became PM.
- First (1754–1756) during the reign of George 2nd when he precipitated the *Seven Years' War*, but his weak diplomacy cost him the premiership and he was succeeded by **William Cavendish, 4th Duke of Devonshire** (Fig. 9.5).
- Second (1757–1762) during the reigns of George 2nd and George 3rd and was succeeded by **John Stuart, Earl of Bute** (Fig. 9.6).
- He died in 1768, aged 75.

(Fig. 9.4)    *(Fig. 9.5)*    *(Fig. 9.6)*

WILLIAM PITT (THE ELDER), 1st EARL OF CHATHAM

(Fig. 9.7)

- William Pitt (1708–1778) was PM during the reign of George 3rd; he was called 'Pitt of Chatham', or 'William Pitt the Elder' to distinguish him from his son,' William Pitt the Younger', who also was a PM.
- In 1735, he first entered the Commons as Whig MP for *Old Sarum*.
- He was PM (1766–1768) and was succeeded by **Augustus FitzRoy, 3rd Duke of Grafton**.
- Pitt is best known as the wartime political leader of Britain in the *Seven Years' War* especially for his single-minded devotion to victory over France.
- He is also known for his popular appeal, his opposition to corruption in government, his support for the colonial position in the run-up to the *American War of Independence* as well as his antagonism towards Spain and France.
- He died in 1778, aged 70.

AUGUSTUS FITZROY, 3rd DUKE OF GRAFTON

(Fig. 9.8)

- Augustus Henry FitzRoy (1736–1811) was PM during the reign of George 3rd.
- In 1756, he entered the Commons as a Whig MP for *Boroughbridge.*
- He was PM (1760–1770) and was succeeded by **Frederick North (Lord North)**.
- During his tenure, he was unable to counter increasing challenges to Britain's global dominance following the victory in the Seven Years' War and was also blamed for allowing France to annex Corsica.
- He died in 1811, aged 75.

FREDERICK NORTH, 2ND EARL OF GUILDFORD (LORD NORTH)

(Fig. 9.9)

- Frederick North (1732–1792) was PM during the reign of George 3rd.
- In 1754, he entered the Commons for the first time as a Tory MP for *Banbury*.
- He was PM (1770–1782) and was succeeded by **Charles Watson-Wentworth, 2nd Marquess of Rockingham** (Fig. 9.10).
- During his tenure, he led Great Britain through most of the *American War of Independence.*
- He died in 1792, aged 60.

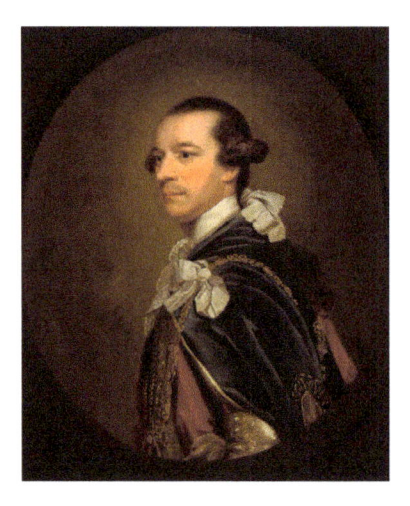

(Fig. 9.10)

WILLIAM PITT (THE YOUNGER)

(Fig. 9.11)

- William Pitt the Younger (1759–1806) was in PM during the reign of George 3rd and became the youngest PM in 1783 at the age of 24; born William Pitt, he is known as 'the Younger' to distinguish him from his father, 'William Pitt the Elder', who had previously served as PM.
- In 1781, he entered the Commons for the first time as MP for *Cambridge University,* and although often referred to as a Tory or 'new Tory', he called himself an 'independent Whig'.
- He served as a PM three times; first as PM of *Great Britain* and then twice as PM of the *United Kingdom*:
- First (1783–1801), and was succeeded by **William Cavendish Bendick, 3rd Duke of Portland** (Fig. 9.12).

(Fig. 9.12)

(Fig. 9.13)   *(Fig. 9.14)*

- Second (Jan–March 1801) and was succeeded by **Henry Addington, 1st Viscount Sidmouth** (Fig. 9.13).
- Third (1804–1806), succeeded by **William Grenville, 1st Baron Grenville** (Fig. 9.14).
- Pitt the Younger is best known for leading Britain in the great wars against France and Napoleon. He was an outstanding administrator who worked for efficiency and reform, bringing in a new generation of outstanding administrators.
- To meet the threat of Irish support for France, he engineered the *Acts of Union* (1800) and tried (but failed) to get Catholic emancipation as part of the Union.
- Pitt created the '*new Toryism*', which revived the Tory Party and enabled it to stay in power for the next quarter-century.
- Pitt died in office in 1806, aged 46.

SPENCER PERCEVAL

(Fig. 9.15)

- Spencer Perceval (1762–1812) was PM during the reign of George 3rd and is the only PM to have been assassinated.
- In 1796 first entered the Commons as MP for *Northampton* and always described himself as a '*friend of Mr Pitt*' rather than a Tory.
- He was PM (1809–1812) and was succeeded by **Robert Jenkinson, 2nd Earl of Liverpool.**
- During his tenure, he was opposed to Catholic emancipation and supported the war against Napoleon and the abolition of the slave trade.
- Percival also pursued the *Peninsula War* in the face of opposition defeatism.
- His position was looking stronger by the spring of 1812 (aged 49), when he was assassinated by **John Bellingham** (Fig. 9.16).

(Fig. 9.16)

ROBERT JENKINSON, 2nd EARL OF LIVERPOOL

(Fig. 9.17)

- Robert Banks Jenkinson (1770–1828) was PM during the reigns of George 3rd and George 4th. In 1790, he first entered the Commons as Tory MP for *Rye*.
- He was PM (1812–1827) and was succeeded by **George Canning**.
- During his tenure as PM, Liverpool dealt smoothly with the Prince Regent when King George 3rd was incapacitated.
- He also steered the country through the period of radicalism and unrest that followed the *Napoleonic Wars* and sought a compromise of the heated issue of Catholic emancipation.
- By the 1820s, he was the leader of a reform faction of '*Liberal Tories*' who lowered the tariff and reformed the criminal law.
- Important events during his tenure as PM included: the *War of 1812* with the United States, the Sixth and Seventh Coalitions against France, and the conclusion of the *Napoleonic Wars* at the Congress of Vienna.
- He died in 1828, aged 58.

GEORGE CANNING

(Fig. 9.18)

- George Canning (1770–1827) was PM and Foreign Secretary during the reign of George 4th.
- In 1793, he first entered the Commons as Tory MP for *Newtown* on the Isle of Wight.
- He was PM (April–Aug. 1827) when Lord Liverpool resigned and he was chosen ahead of the **Duke of Wellington** and **Sir Robert Peel** who declined to serve under him. The Tories split between Peel and Wellington's '*Ultra-Tories*' and the '*Canningites*'; he was succeeded by **Frederick John Robinson, 1st Viscount Goderich** (Fig. 9.19).

(Fig. 9.19)

- Canning was the dominant figure in the cabinet and directed the seizure of the Danish fleet in 1807 to assure Britain's naval supremacy over Napoleon.
- The King disliked Canning, but he successfully built wide public support for his policies that ensured a major trading advantage to British merchants and supported the United States' *Monroe Doctrine*.
- Canning died in August 1827, aged 57, after just 119 days in office—the shortest tenure of any British PM.

ARTHUR WELLESLEY, 1ST DUKE OF WELLINGTON

(Fig. 9.20)

- Arthur Wellesley (1769–1852) was PM during the reigns of George 4th and William 4th.
- In 1806, he first entered the Commons as Tory MP for *Rye*.
- He was PM on two occasions.
- First (1828–1830), during the reigns of George 4th and William 4th and was succeeded by **Frederick John Robinson, 1st Viscount Goderich**.
- Second (Nov.–Dec. 1834), during the reign of William 4th and was succeeded by **Sir Robert Peel**.
- Wellington also had an illustrious military career prior to entering politics (*see* Chapter 10).

WILLIAM LAMB, 2nd VISCOUNT MELBOURNE

(Fig. 9.21)

- William Lamb (1779–1848) was PM during the reign of William 4th and then Queen Victoria.
- In 1806, he first entered the Commons as Whig MP for *Leominster*.
- He was PM on two occasions:
- First (July–Nov. 1834) during the reign of William 4th; the King dismissed him and replaced him by the **Duke of Wellington**.
- Second (1835–1841) during the reigns of William 4th and Queen Victoria; he was succeeded by **Sir Robert Peel**.
- Melbourne is best known for his successful mentoring of the young Queen Victoria in the ways of politics but is not ranked highly as a PM, as there were no great foreign wars or domestic issues to handle.
- He died in 1848, aged 69.

SIR ROBERT PEEL, 2nd BARONET

(Fig. 9.22)

- Robert Peel (1788–1850) was PM during the reigns of William 4th and then Queen Victoria.
- In 1809, he first entered the Commons as Tory MP for the borough of *Cashel*.
- He was PM on two occasions:
- First (1834–1835), during the reign of William 4th and was succeeded by **William Lamb, 2nd Viscount Melbourne**.
- Second (1841–1846), during the reign of Queen Victoria and was succeeded by **Lord John Russell**.
- Peel is regarded as the father of modern British policing and as one of the founders of the modern Conservative Party.
- He entered the Cabinet for the first time as Home Secretary (1822–1827) and created the modern police force.
- In 1830, the Whigs finally returned to power and Peel became a member of the opposition for the first time.
- After successive election defeats, leadership of the Conservative Party gradually passed from Wellington to Peel, and when King William 4th asked Wellington to become PM in November 1834, he declined and Peel was selected instead, with Wellington serving as caretaker until Peel took office.

- After the outbreak of the *Great Irish Potato Famine*, Peel's decision to join with the Whigs and the Radicals to repeal the *Corn Laws* led to his resignation in 1846.
- Peel remained an influential backbencher and leader of the Peelite faction until his death in 1850, aged 62.

JOHN RUSSELL, 1st EARL RUSSELL

(Fig. 9.23)

- John Russell (1792–1878) was PM during the reign of Queen Victoria.
- In 1813, he first entered the Commons as a Whig MP for *Tavistock*.
- He was PM on two occasions:
- First (1846–1852) and was succeeded by **Edward Smith-Stanley, 14th Earl of Derby.**
- Second (1865–1866) and was also succeeded by **Lord Derby**.
- During his tenure, he failed to deal with the famine in Ireland that caused the loss of a quarter of its population.
- His first government (1846–1852) was the ruin of the Whig party, and the second (1865–1866) might be described as the first Liberal Government and was also very nearly the ruin of the Liberal party.
- He died in 1878, aged 85.

EDWARD SMITH-STANLEY, 14th EARL OF DERBY

(Fig. 9.24)

- Edward George Geoffrey Smith-Stanley (1799-1869) was PM during the reign of Queen Victoria.
- In 1822, he first entered the Commons as a Whig MP for the borough of *Stockbridge*.
- He was PM on three occasions:
- First (Feb.-Dec. 1852), and was succeeded by **George Hamilton-Gordon, 4th Earl of Aberdeen** (Fig. 9.25).
- Second (1858-1859), and was succeeded by **Henry John Temple, 3rd Viscount Palmerston**.
- Third (1866-1868), and was succeeded by **Benjamin Disraeli, 1st Earl of Beaconsfield**.

(Fig. 9.25)

- To date, he is one of only four PMs to have had three or more separate periods in office.
- However, his ministries all lasted less than two years, and totalled three years 280 days.
- His greatest achievement was to create the modern Conservative Party in the framework of the Whig constitution.
- He died in 1869, aged 70.

HENRY JOHN TEMPLE, 3rd VISCOUNT PALMERSTON

(Fig. 9.26)

- Henry John Temple (1784–1865) was PM during the reign of Queen Victoria.
- In 1806, he first entered the Commons as Tory MP for *Horsham*.
- He was PM on two occasions:
- First (1855–1858) and was succeeded by **Edward Smith-Stanley, 14th Earl of Derby**.
- Second (1859–1865) and was succeeded by **Lord John Russell**.
- Although Palmerston began his parliamentary career as a Tory, he switched to the Whigs in 1830, and then from 1859 became the first PM of the newly-formed Liberal Party.
- Between 1830 and 1865, Palmerston dominated foreign policy when Britain was at the height of her power and is regarded as one of the greatest of foreign secretaries.
- He died in office in 1865, aged 81.

BENJAMIN DISRAELI, 1st EARL OF BEACONSFIELD

(Fig. 9.27)

- Benjamin Disraeli (1804–1881) was PM during the reign of Queen Victoria.
- In 1837, he first entered the Commons as Tory MP for *Maidstone*.
- By 1846, had become a major figure and served as Chancellor of the Exchequer and Leader of the House of Commons.
- He was PM on two occasions:
- First (Feb.–Dec. 1868), and was succeeded by **William Gladstone**.
- Second (1874–1880), and was again succeeded by **William Gladstone**.
- He played a central role in the creation of the modern Conservative party, and is remembered for his political battles with the Liberal Party leader William Gladstone.
- Disraeli maintained a close friendship with Queen Victoria who created him Earl of Beaconsfield.
- Disraeli's second term was dominated by the slow decay of the Ottoman Empire and the desire of other European powers, such as Russia, to gain at its expense.
- In 1878, his diplomatic victory at the Congress of Berlin over Russia established Disraeli as one of Europe's leading statesmen.
- Throughout his career Disraeli had written novels, and he published his last entitled *Endymion* shortly before he died in 1881, aged 76.

WILLIAM GLADSTONE

(Fig. 9.28)

- William Ewart Gladstone (1809–1898) was PM during the reign of Queen Victoria.
- In 1832, he first entered the Commons as Tory MP for *Greenwich*, and then, after the split of the Tories, he became a Peelite until 1859 when they merged with the Whigs and Radicals to form the new Liberal Party.
- He was PM on four occasions:
- First (1868–1874), and was succeeded by **Benjamin Disraeli**.
- Second (1880–1885), and was succeeded by **Robert Gascoyne-Cecil, 3rd Marquess of Salisbury.**
- Third (Feb.–July 1886), and was succeeded by the **Marquess of Salisbury**.
- Fourth (1892–1894), and was succeeded by **Archibald Primrose, 5th Earl of Rosebery** (Fig. 9.29).

(Fig. 9.29)

- After his electoral defeat in 1874, Gladstone resigned as leader of the Liberal Party, but from 1876 he began a comeback.
- Back in office in early 1886, he proposed Irish home rule but this was defeated in the House of Commons in July.
- The resulting split in the Liberal Party helped keep them out of office, with one short break, for twenty years.
- In 1892, Gladstone formed his last government at the age of 82 but resigned in March 1894 and left Parliament the following year.
- He died in 1898, aged 88.

ROBERT GASCOYNE-CECIL, 3rd MARQUESS OF SALISBURY

(Fig. 9.30)

- Robert Arthur Talbot Gascoyne-Cecil (1830–1903) was PM during the reigns of Queen Victoria and Edward 7th.
- In 1853, he first entered the Commons as Tory MP for *Stamford*.
- He was PM on three occasions:
- First (1885–1886), during the reign of Queen Victoria and was succeeded by **William Gladstone**.

- Second (1886–92) during the reign of Queen Victoria and was again succeeded by **William Gladstone**.
- Third (1895–1902) during the reigns of Queen Victoria and then Edward 7th and was succeeded by his nephew, **Arthur Balfour**.
- In 1868, upon the death of his father, Gascoyne-Cecil was elevated to the House of Lords and became Conservative leader of the Lords with **Sir Stafford Northcote** (Fig. 9.31) leading the party in the Commons.
- He died in 1903, aged 73.

(Fig. 9.31)

ARTHUR BALFOUR, 1st EARL OF BALFOUR

(Fig. 9.32)

- Arthur James Balfour (1848–1930) was PM during the reign of Edward 7th.
- In 1874, he first entered the Commons as Tory MP for *Hertford*.
- He was PM (1902– 1905) and was succeeded by **Sir Henry Campbell-Bannerman**.
- During his tenure, he secured the Entente Cordiale with France, leaving Germany in the cold.
- In 1905, he resigned as PM and in the elections the following year he lost his parliamentary seat but re-entered Parliament at a by-election.
- In 1911, he resigned as party leader but returned as First Lord of the Admiralty in Asquith's Coalition Government (1915–1916).
- In December 1916, he became Foreign Secretary in Lloyd George's coalition, but was frequently left out of the inner workings of foreign policy, although the *Balfour Declaration* on a Jewish homeland bore his name.
- He continued to serve in senior positions throughout the 1920s.
- He died in 1930, aged 81.

HENRY CAMPBELL-BANNERMAN

(Fig. 9.33)

- Sir Henry Campbell-Bannerman (1836–1908) was PM during the reign of Edward 7th.

- In 1868, he first entered the Commons as Liberal MP for *Stirling Burghs*.
- He was PM (1905–1908) and was succeeded by **H. H. Asquith**.
- Following a general election defeat in 1900, Campbell–Bannerman went on to lead the Liberal Party to a landslide victory over the Conservatives, and at the 1906 elections, the Liberals gained an overall majority in the House of Commons.
- In April 1908, Campbell–Bannerman resigned as PM due to ill health and died several days later aged, 71.

EDWARD GREY, 1st VISCOUNT GREY OF FALLODON

(Fig. 9.34)

- Edward Grey (1862–1933), better known as Sir Edward Grey, was Foreign Secretary (1905–1916) during the reigns of Edward 7th and George 6th.
- In 1885, he entered the Commons as Liberal MP for *Berwick-upon-Tweed*.
- He is best remembered for his '*lamps are going out*' remark on 3rd August 1914 on the outbreak of the First World War.
- Ennobled in 1916, he was Ambassador to Washington (1919–1920) and Leader of the Liberal Party in the House of Lords (1923–1924).

H. H. ASQUITH, 1st EARL OF OXFORD AND ASQUITH

(Fig. 9.35)

- Herbert Henry Asquith (1852–1928) was PM during the reigns of Edward 7th and George 5th.
- In 1886, he first entered the Commons as Liberal MP for *East Fife*.
- He was PM (1908–1916) and was succeeded by **David Lloyd George**.
- In August 1914, he took the United Kingdom into WW1, but setbacks in the war forced him to form a coalition government with the Conservatives and Labour early in 1915.
- Bitter rivalries inside and between the three major parties worsened when Asquith was unable to forge the coalition into a harmonious team.
- In December 1916, Lloyd George organised his overthrow and replaced him as PM.
- Asquith remained as leader of the Liberal Party but was unable to quell the internal conflict and the party rapidly declined.
- In 1925, he accepted a peerage and died in 1928, aged 75.

DAVID LLOYD GEORGE, 1st EARL LLOYD-GEORGE OF DWYFOR

(Fig. 9.36) *(Fig. 9.37)*

- David Lloyd George (1863–1945) was PM during the reign of George 5th.
- In 1890, he first entered the Commons as Liberal MP for *Carnarvon Buroughs*.
- He was PM (1916–1922) of the Wartime Coalition Government and immediately after, and was succeeded by **Andrew Bonar Law**.
- Lloyd George was a major player at the *Paris Peace Conference* (1919) (Fig. 9.37) that reordered Europe after the defeat of the Central Powers, and played a dominant role in winning WW1.
- He became leader of the Liberal Party in the late 1920s, but it grew even smaller and more divided, and by the 1930s he was a marginalised and widely mistrusted figure.
- He gave weak support to WW2 amidst fears that he was favourable toward Germany.
- He died in 1945, aged 82.

RAMSAY MACDONALD

(Fig. 9.38)

- James Ramsay MacDonald (1866–1937) was PM during the reign of George 5th.
- He was the first Labour PM and is credited, along with **Keir Hardie** (Fig. 9.39) and **Arthur Henderson** (Fig. 9.40), as one of the three principal founders of the Labour Party.

(Fig. 9.39)    *(Fig. 9.40)*

- In 1906, he first entered the Commons as Labour MP for *Seaham*.
- He was PM on two occasions:
- First (Jan.–Nov. 1924), and was succeeded by **Stanley Baldwin**.
- Second (1929–1931), and then (1931–1935) as leader of the National Government, and was also succeeded by **Stanley Baldwin**.

- In 1931, MacDonald formed a National Government in which only two of his Labour colleagues agreed to serve; his majority came from the Conservatives.
- The National coalition won an overwhelming victory at the elections and the Labour Party was reduced to about 50 seats in the House of Commons.
- MacDonald was expelled from the Labour Party, but remained PM of the National Government.
- He died in 1937, aged 71, still an MP.

STANLEY BALDWIN, 1st EARL BALDWIN OF BEWDLEY

(Fig. 9.41)

- Stanley Baldwin (1867–1947) was PM during the reigns of George 5th, Edward 8th and George 6th.
- In 1908, he first entered the Commons as Conservative MP *for Bewdley*.
- He was PM on three occasions:
- First (1923–1924) during the reign of George 5th and was succeeded by **Ramsay MacDonald**.

- Second (1924–1929) also during the reign of George 5th and was succeeded by **Ramsey MacDonald**.
- Third (1935–1937) during the reigns of Edward 8th and George 6th and was succeeded by **Neville Chamberlain**.
- In 1924, the Conservatives won the general election and Baldwin formed his second government, which saw important tenures of office by **Sir Austen Chamberlain** (Foreign Secretary) (Fig. 9.42), **Winston Churchill** (Chancellor of the Exchequer) and **Neville Chamberlain** (Health).

(Fig. 9.42)

- In 1929, Baldwin narrowly lost the general election, and in 1931, Labour Prime Minister, Ramsey MacDonald, formed a National Government and Baldwin took over many of the PM's duties due to MacDonald's failing health, and in 1935, he replaced MacDonald as PM and won the general election with a large majority.
- During this time, he oversaw the beginning of the rearmament process of the British military as well as the very difficult abdication of **King Edward 8th**.
- Baldwin's third government saw several crises in foreign affairs, including the public uproar over the *Hoare–Laval Pact*, Hitler's re-occupation of the Rhineland and the outbreak of the *Spanish Civil War*.
- Baldwin retired in 1937, and died ten years later, aged 80.

NEVILLE CHAMBERLAIN

(Fig. 9.43)

- Arthur Neville Chamberlain (1869–1940) was PM during the reign of George 6th.
- In 1918, he first entered the Commons as Conservative MP for *Birmingham, Ladywood.*
- He was PM (1937–1940) and was succeeded by **Winston Churchill**.
- His tenure is best known for his appeasement foreign policy and in particular for his signing of the *Munich Agreement* in 1938 (Fig. 9.44) conceding the German-speaking Sudetenland region of Czechoslovakia to Germany.
- However, when Adolf Hitler later invaded Poland, the UK declared war on Germany on 3rd September 1939, and Chamberlain led Britain through the first eight months of WW2.

(Fig. 9.44)

- Chamberlain resigned as PM on 10th May 1940, as he believed a government supported by all parties was essential and the Labour and Liberal parties would not join a government headed by him.
- **Winston Churchill** took over as PM, but Chamberlain remained an important member of the Cabinet before resigning due to ill health and dying of cancer aged 71.

EDWARD WOOD, 1st EARL OF HALIFAX

(Fig. 9.45)

- Edward Frederick Lindley Wood (1881–1959) was Foreign Secretary during the reign of George 6th.
- In 1910, he first entered the Commons as Conservative MP for *Ripon* and held the seat until his elevation to the Lords in 1925.
- He was Foreign Secretary (1938–1940) and was succeeded by **Anthony Eden**.
- Halifax is regarded as one of the architects of appeasement prior to WW2 although, after Hitler's occupation of the rump of Czechoslovakia in March 1939, he attempted to deter further German aggression by promising to go to war to defend Poland.
- In May 1940, on Neville Chamberlain's resignation, Halifax declined the position of PM despite widespread support, as he felt that Churchill would be a more suitable war leader.
- He then served as Ambassador in Washington (1940–1946) and died in 1959, aged 71.

WINSTON CHURCHILL

(Fig. 9.46)

- Sir Winston Leonard Spencer–Churchill (1874–1965) was PM during the reigns of George 6th and then Elizabeth 2nd. Churchill was born into the family of the Dukes of Marlborough, a branch of the Spencer Family.
- His father, *Lord Randolph Churchill,* was a charismatic politician who served as Chancellor of the Exchequer and his mother, *Jennie Jerome,* was an American socialite.
- In 1900, he first entered the Commons as Conservative MP for *Oldham*, but four years later, he crossed the floor to sit as a member of the Liberal Party.
- As a young army officer (Fig. 9.47), he saw action in India, the *Anglo-Sudan War,* and the *Second Boer War,* and he gained fame as a war correspondent and wrote books about his campaigns.
- During WW1, he was First Lord of the Admiralty until the disastrous *Gallipoli Campaign* caused him to resign.
- He then briefly resumed active army service on the Western Front as commander of the 6th Battalion of the Royal Scots Fusiliers.

(Fig. 9.47)

- He returned to government under **Lloyd George** and held several posts, and then after two years out of Parliament, he served as Chancellor of the Exchequer in **Baldwin's** Conservative government (1924–1929).
- Out of office and politically '*in the wilderness*' during the 1930s because of his opposition to increased home rule for India and his resistance to the 1936 abdication of King Edward 8th, Churchill took the lead in warning about Germany and in campaigning for rearmament.
- He was PM on two occasions:
- First (1940–1945), during the reign of George 6th and was succeeded by **Clement Attlee**.
- Second (1951–1955), during the reigns of George 6th and Elizabeth 2nd, and was succeeded by **Anthony Eden**.
- At the outbreak of WW2, he was again appointed First Lord of the Admiralty, and following the resignation of **Neville Chamberlain** on 10th May 1940, Churchill became PM until victory had been secured.
- After the Conservative Party suffered an unexpected defeat in the 1945 general election, he became Leader of the Opposition, and publicly warned of an '*Iron Curtain*' of Soviet influence descending over Europe.
- In 1951, Churchill again became PM and was preoccupied by foreign affairs.
- In 1953, he suffered a stroke and in 1955 he retired as PM.
- He remained a MP until 1964 and died the following year, aged 90.

CLEMENT ATTLEE, 1st EARL ATTLEE

(Fig. 9.48)

- Clement Richard Attlee (1883–1967) was PM during the reign of George 6th.
- In 1922, he first entered the Commons as Labour MP for *Limehouse.*
- He rose quickly to become a junior minister in the minority government led by **Ramsey MacDonald** in 1924 and then joined the Cabinet during MacDonald's second ministry (1929–1931). He was one of only a handful of Labour frontbenchers to retain his seat in the landslide defeat of 1931.
- In 1935, he became the Leader of the Labour Party and, at first, he advocated appeasement but later reversed his position and by 1938 became a strong critic of **Neville Chamberlain's** attempts to appease Adolf Hitler.
- He was Deputy PM (1942–1945) in the coalition government during WW2 and worked smoothly with Churchill and was succeeded by **Herbert Morrison** (Fig. 9.49).

(Fig. 9.49)

- With victory in Europe in May 1945, the coalition government was dissolved, and Attlee led Labour to win a huge majority in the ensuing 1945 general election two months later.
- He was PM (1945–1951) and was succeeded by **Winston Churchill**.
- In 1955, he was elevated to the House of Lords and died in 1967, aged 84.

ANTHONY EDEN, 1st EARL OF AVON

(Fig. 9.50)

- Robert Anthony Eden (1897–1977) was in office as Foreign Secretary during the reign of George 6th and then as PM during the reign of Elizabeth 2nd.
- In 1923, he first entered the Commons as Conservative MP *Warwick* and *Leamington*.
- In 1935, at the age of 38, he became Foreign Secretary before resigning in 1938 in protest at Neville Chamberlain's appeasement policy towards Mussolini.
- He again became Foreign Secretary for most of WW2 and a third time in 1951.
- Having been Winston Churchill's deputy forfor almost 15 years, he succeeded him as PM in 1955 and a month later won the general election.

- He was PM (1955–1957) and was succeeded by **Harold Macmillan**.
- His tenure and reputation were overshadowed in 1956 when the United States refused to support the Anglo–French military response to the *Suez Crisis*, which signalled the end British predominance in the Middle East.
- In 1957, he resigned as PM on grounds of ill health and because he was widely suspected of having misled the House of Commons over the degree of 'collusion' with France and Israel.
- He died in 1977, aged 80.

HAROLD MACMILLAN, 1ST EARL OF STOCKTON

(Fig. 9.51)

- Maurice Harold Macmillan (1894–1986) was PM during the reign of Elizabeth 2nd.
- He served in the Grenadier Guards during WW1 and was wounded several times.
- In 1924, he first entered the Commons as Conservative MP for *Stockton-on-Tees*.
- Under Anthony Eden, he served as Foreign Secretary and Chancellor of the Exchequer.
- He was PM (1957–1963) and was succeeded by **Sir Alec Douglas-Home** (Fig. 9.52).

(Fig. 9.52)

- During his tenure, Macmillan presided over an age of affluence marked by low unemployment and high, if uneven, growth, and told the nation that they had *'never had it so good'*.
- In 1959, the Conservatives were re-elected with an increased majority and Macmillan rebuilt the special relationship with the United States from the wreckage of the *Suez Crisis*, although near the end of his premiership, his government was rocked by the Vassall and Profumo scandals.
- Macmillan lived out a long retirement as an elder statesman and died in 1986, aged 92.

HAROLD WILSON, BARON OF RIEVAULX

(Fig. 9.53)

- James Harold Wilson (1916–1995) was PM during the reign of Elizabeth 2nd.
- In 1945, he first entered the Commons as Labour MP for *Omskirk*.
- In 1963, he was elected Leader of the Labour Party after the sudden death of **Hugh Gaitskell** (Fig. 9.54).
- He was PM on two occasions:
- First (1964–1970) and was succeeded by **Edward Heath**.
- Second (1974–1976) and was succeeded by **James Callaghan** (Fig. 9.55).
- Wilson's first term as PM coincided with a period of low unemployment and relative economic prosperity.
- In 1970, he lost the general election to Edward Heath and spent four years as Leader of the Opposition.

(Fig. 9.54)    *(Fig. 9.55)*

- In 1974, Wilson returned to power as leader of a minority government until a second election later that year resulted in a narrow Labour victory.
- In 1976, he suddenly resigned as PM probably due to ill–health, and died in 1995, aged 79.

EDWARD HEATH

(Fig. 9.56)

- Sir Edward Richard George Heath (1916–2005), often known as 'Ted' Heath, was PM during the reign of Elizabeth 2nd.
- In 1950, he first entered the Commons as Conservative MP for *Bexley*.
- He was PM (1970–1974) and was succeeded by **Harold Wilson**.
- In January 1973, Heath negotiated Britain's entry into the EU but his government foundered on economic difficulties – including high inflation and major strikes that he could not control.
- In 1974, the party was defeated by Labour and he became a vehement opponent of **Margaret Thatcher** who succeeded him as party leader in 1975.
- He returned to the backbenches and remained an MP until 2001.
- He died in 2005, aged 79.

Politicians | 155

MARGARET THATCHER, BARONESS THATCHER OF KESTEVEN

(Fig. 9.57)

- Margaret Hilda Thatcher (1925–2013) was PM during the reign of Elizabeth 2nd; she was the longest-serving PM of the 20th century and the first woman to have held the office.
- In 1959, she first entered the Commons as Conservative MP for *Finchley*.
- In 1975, Thatcher defeated Heath and became Leader of the Conservative party as well as leader of the opposition.
- She was PM (1979–1990) and was succeeded by **John Major** (Fig. 9.58).

(Fig. 9.58)

- During her tenure, she introduced a series of political and economic initiatives intended to reverse high unemployment and recession.
- Thatcher's popularity waned during her first years in office until victory in the *Falklands War* (1982), and the Conservatives were re-elected in 1983 and 1987.
- In November 1990, she resigned as PM and party leader after **Michael Heseltine** (Fig. 9.59) launched a challenge to her leadership.

(Fig. 9.59)

- In 1992, she retired from the House of Commons and was awarded a life peerage.
- In 2002, after a series of small strokes, she withdrew from public speaking.
- In 2013, she died aged 87.

TONY BLAIR

(Fig. 9.60)

- Anthony Charles Lynton Blair (b. 1953) was PM during the reign of Elizabeth 2nd.
- In 1983, he first entered the Commons as Labour MP for *Sedgefield*.
- In July 1994, he became leader of the Labour Party following the sudden death of **John Smith**.
- Under Blair's leadership, the party used the phrase '*New Labour*' to distance it from the traditional conception of socialism.
- Critics denounced him for having the Labour Party abandon genuine socialism and accepting capitalism, while supporters argued that, after four consecutive general election defeats, the Labour Party had to demonstrate that it had made a decisive break from its left-wing past in order to win an election again.
- He was PM (1997–2007) and was succeeded by **Gordon Brown** (Fig. 9.61).
- The landslide general election victory in 1997 was the largest in history, and allowed Blair, aged 43, to become the youngest PM since 1812.
- The Labour Party went on to win two more elections (2001 and 2005) under his leadership.
- Blair strongly supported the foreign policy of Bush's American administration and ensured that the British Armed Forces participated

(Fig. 9.61)

in the invasion of Afghanistan (2001), and more controversially, the invasion of Iraq (2003).
- Blair faced strong criticism for his role in the invasion of Iraq, and in 2016, the Iraq Inquiry strongly criticised his actions and described them as 'unjustified and unnecessary'.

10
NOTABLE MILITARY COMMANDERS

JOHN CHURCHILL, 1st DUKE OF MARLBOROUGH

(Fig. 10.1)

- General John Churchill (1650–1722) was an *army officer* whose career spanned the reigns of five monarchs.
- He served **James** (Duke of York – later King James 2nd) through the 1670s and early 1680s. Churchill's role in defeating the *Monmouth Rebellion* (1685) helped secure James on the throne, yet just three years later, he abandoned his Catholic patron for the Protestant Dutchman, **William of Orange**.
- At William's coronation, Churchill was awarded the earldom of Marlborough and served with further distinction during the early years of the Nine Years' War.
- It was not until the accession of **Queen Anne** (1702) that Marlborough reached the zenith of his powers.
- His marriage to the hot-tempered **Sarah** (Fig. 10.2), the Queen's intimate friend, ensured Marlborough's rise to a dukedom and he received Blenheim Palace (Fig. 10.3) as a gift.

(Fig. 10.2)

(Fig. 10.3)

- During the *War of the Spanish Succession*, Marlborough became *de facto* leader of the Allied forces against the French. His victories at *Blenheim* (1704), *Ramillies* (1706), *Oudenarde* (1708), and *Malplaquet* (1709) (Fig. 10.4) ensured his place in history.
- His wife's stormy relationship with the Queen and her subsequent dismissal from court, was the main cause of his fall from office and self-imposed exile.

(Fig. 10.4)

- In 1714, Marlborough returned to England when **King George 1st** acceded to the throne.
- Throughout ten consecutive campaigns during the *War of the Spanish Succession*, Marlborough held together a coalition and his victories allowed Britain to rise from a minor to a major power.
- He died in 1722, aged 72.

HORATIO NELSON, 1ST VISCOUNT NELSON

(Fig. 10.5)

- Horatio Nelson (1758–1805) was a *naval officer*.
- Nelson rose rapidly through the ranks in the navy and obtained his own command in 1778. During the *French Revolutionary Wars*, he was active in the Mediterranean.
- In 1797, he distinguished himself at the *Battle of Cape St. Vincent*, and shortly after took part in the *Battle of Santa Cruz de Tenerife*, where he lost his right arm.
- The following year, he won a decisive victory over the French at the *Battle of the Nile* (Fig. 10.6), and in 1801 he was victorious at the *Battle of Copenhagen*.
- In 1805, he took over the Cadiz blockade and later that year engaged

the Franco–Spanish fleet as it came out of port at the *Battle of Trafalgar* (Fig. 10.7).
- Trafalgar was Britain's greatest naval victory, but during the action, Nelson, aboard *HMS Victory* was fatally wounded (Fig. 10.8) and he died aged 47.

(Fig. 10.6)

(Fig. 10.7)

(Fig. 10.8)

ARTHUR WELLESLEY, 1st DUKE OF WELLINGTON

(Fig. 10.9)

- Field Marshal Arthur Wellesley (1769–1852) was *an army officer* and a *statesman*.
- He was twice Prime Minister (*see* chapter 9).
- In 1796, as a colonel, he saw action in the Netherlands and in India, where he fought in the Fourth Anglo–Mysore War at the *Battle of Seringapatam*.

(Fig. 10.10)

- In 1799, he won a decisive victory at the *Battle of Assaye* (1803) (Fig. 10.10).
- Wellesley rose to prominence as a general during the *Peninsular Campaign* of the Napoleonic Wars and was promoted to field marshal after leading his forces to victory against the French at the *Battle of Vitoria* (1813).
- In 1814, following **Napoleon's** exile, he served as ambassador to Paris and was granted a dukedom.
- In 1815, during the *Hundred Days War*, he commanded the combined armies of Britain and Prussia, which defeated Napoleon at the *Battle of Waterloo* (Fig. 10.11).
- Wellington is regarded as one of the greatest defensive commanders of all time.
- After ending his active military career, he returned to politics and was Prime Minister on two occasions (*see* Chapter 9).
- He remained Commander-in-Chief of the British Army until his death in 1852, aged 83.

(Fig. 10.11)

CHARLES GORDON

(Fig. 10.12)

- Major General Charles George Gordon (1833–1885), also known as 'Chinese Gordon', and 'Gordon of Khartoum', was an *army officer* and *administrator*.
- He saw action in the *Crimean War* but made his military reputation in China.
- In the early 1860s, Gordon was instrumental in putting down the *Taiping Rebellion* and received honours from both the Emperor of China and the British.
- In 1873, he entered the service of the Khedive of Egypt and later became the Governor General of Sudan.
- A revolt then broke out in the Sudan, led by a Muslim religious leader and self-proclaimed Mahdi, **Muhammad Ahmad.** In early 1884, Gordon was sent to Khartoum to secure the evacuation of loyal soldiers and civilians.
- However, after evacuating about 2,500 British civilians, he retained a smaller group of soldiers and non-military men.

- In the build-up to battle, the two leaders corresponded, each attempting to convert the other to his faith, but neither would accede.
- Besieged by the Mahdi's forces, Gordon organised a citywide defence lasting almost a year. This gained him the admiration of the British public, but not of the government.
- Only when public pressure to act had become irresistible did the government, with reluctance, send a relief force. However, it arrived two days after the city had fallen and Gordon had been killed (Fig. 10.13).

(Fig. 10.13)

HERBERT KITCHENER, 1st EARL KITCHENER

(Fig. 10.14)

- Field Marshal Horatio Herbert Kitchener (1850–1916) was an *army officer* and a *statesman*.
- In 1898, he won the *Battle of Omdurman* (Fig. 10.15) and secured control of the Sudan, after which he was given the title 'Lord Kitchener of Khartoum'.

(Fig. 10.15)

- As Chief of Staff (1900–1902) in the *Second Boer War*, he played a key role in Lord Roberts' conquest of the Boer Republics.
- He then succeeded Roberts as Commander-in-Chief – by which time the Boer forces had taken to guerrilla fighting and the British imprisoned Boer civilians in concentration camps.
- During his term as Commander-in-Chief in India (1902–1909), he quarrelled with Viceroy **Lord Curzon** (Fig. 10.16), who eventually resigned.

(Fig. 10.16)

- Kitchener then returned to Egypt as British Agent and Consul-General (*de facto* administrator).
- In 1914, at the start of WW1, Kitchener became Secretary of State for War, and was one of the few to foresee a long war, organising the largest volunteer army that Britain had seen.
- Despite having warned of the difficulty of provisioning Britain for a long war, he was blamed for the shortage of shells in the spring of 1915 and was stripped of his control over munitions and strategy.
- Kitchener died on 5th June 1916, aged 66, when *HMS Hampshire* sank west of the Orkney Islands after striking a German mine. He was on his way to Russia to attend negotiations and was one of more than 600 to die.

EDMUND ALLENBY, 1st VISCOUNT ALLENBY

(Fig. 10.17)

- Field Marshal Edmund Henry Hynman Allenby (1861–1936) was an *army officer* and an *imperial governor*.
- He fought in the *Second Boer War* and also in WW1, during which time he commanded the British Empire's Egyptian Expeditionary Force during the *Sinai and Palestine Campaign* against the Ottoman Empire in the conquest of Palestine.
- The British succeed in capturing Beersheba, Jaffa, and Jerusalem (Oct.–Dec. 1917).
- During the summer of 1918, his forces occupied the Jordan Valley, captured northern Palestine, and defeated the Ottomans at the *Battle of Megiddo* (Fig. 10.18).
- Subsequently, his forces captured Damascus and advanced into northern Syria.

(Fig. 10.18)

- During this pursuit, he commanded T. E. Lawrence (*"Lawrence of Arabia"*) (Fig. 10.19), whose campaign assisted the British in capturing Turkish territory.

(Fig. 10.19)

- From 1919 until 1925, Allenby served as High Commissioner for Egypt and Sudan.
- He died in 1936, aged 75.

JOHN FRENCH, 1st EARL OF YPRES

(Fig. 10.20)

- Field Marshal John Denton Pinkstone French (1852–1925), was an *army officer*.
- He became a national hero during the *Second Boer War* when he was victorious at the *Battle of Elandslaagte* (Oct. 1899) (Fig. 10.21).

- During 1912, he served as Inspector-General of the Army, before becoming Chief of the Imperial Staff and helping to prepare the British Army for a possible European War.
- During the beginning of WW1, he was Commander-in-Chief of the British Expeditionary Force.
- After the British suffered heavy casualties at the *Battle of Mons* (16th Aug. 1914) and the *Battle of Le Cateau* (24th Aug. 1914), where **General Horace Smith-Dorrien** (Fig. 10.22) made a stand contrary to his wishes, French wanted to withdraw the Expeditionary Force. He only agreed to take part in the *First Battle of the Marne* (Sep. 1914) after a meeting with the Secretary of State for War, **Lord Kitchener.**

(Fig. 10.21)   (Fig. 10.22)

- By summer 1915, French's tenure of command was criticised and after the *Battle of Loos* (Sep. 1916), Prime Minister **H. H. Asquith** demanded his resignation and replaced him with **General Douglas Haig**.
- French was then appointed Commander-in-Chief of the Home Forces (1916-1918).
- While the *Battle of Passchendaele – Third Battle of Ypres* (July-Nov. 1917) (Fig. 10.23) was in progress, French was critical of Haig's command and recommended that there be no further major offensives until the American Expeditionary Force had arrived in strength.
- In 1918, French became Lord Lieutenant of Ireland, a position he held throughout much of the *Irish War of Independence* (1919-1922).
- He died in 1925, aged 73.

(Fig. 10.23)

DOUGLAS HAIG, 1st EARL HAIG

(Fig. 10.24)

- Field Marshal Douglas Haig (1861–1928) was an *army officer*.
- During WW1, he commanded the British Expeditionary Force on the Western Front from late 1916 until the end of the war.
- He was in command during the *Battle of the Somme* (July–Nov. 1916) (Fig. 10.25), the *Battle of Passchendaele – Third Battle of Ypres* (July–Nov. 1917) (*see* Fig. 10.23), and the *Hundred Days Offensive* (Aug.–Nov. 1918).

(Fig. 10.25)

- Although Haig had gained a favourable reputation during the immediate post-war years, since the 1960s he had become an object of criticism and was nicknamed '*Butcher Haig*' for the two million British casualties endured under his command.
- Others have praised Haig's leadership, and since the 1980s, some historians have argued that the public hatred in which Haig's name had come to be held failed to recognise the adoption of new tactics and technologies by forces under his command.
- He died in 1928, aged 67.

HUGH TRENCHARD, 1st VISCOUNT TRENCHARD

(Fig. 10.26)

- Marshal of the RAF Hugh Montague Trenchard (1873–1956) was an *army* and *air force officer* who has been described as the 'Father of the RAF'.
- As a young infantry officer, he served in India. With the outbreak of the *Boer War*, he volunteered for service in South Africa, where he was seriously wounded.
- Trenchard then commanded the South Nigerian Regiment for several years.
- In summer 1912, he learned to fly and was subsequently appointed as second in command of the Central Flying School.
- During WW1, he served as commander of the Royal Flying Corps (Fig. 10.27) in France (1915–1917) and in 1918, he commanded the Independent Air Force.
- In 1919, he became Chief of the Air Staff under Winston Churchill and spent the following decade securing the future of the RAF; he is recognised today as one of the early advocates of strategic bombing.
- He died in 1956, aged 83.

(Fig. 10.27)

JOHN JELLICOE, 1st EARL JELLICOE

(Fig. 10.28)

- Admiral of the Fleet John Rushworth Jellicoe (1859–1935) was a *naval officer*.
- He fought in the *Anglo-Egyptian War* and the *Boxer Rebellion*.
- In May 1916, he commanded the Grand Fleet at the *Battle of Jutland* (Fig. 10.29), but his handling of the fleet was controversial; although he made no serious mistakes, the German Fleet retreated to port at a time when defeat would have been catastrophic for Britain.
- Jellicoe later served as First Sea Lord, overseeing the expansion of the Naval Staff at the Admiralty and the introduction of convoys, but was relieved at the end of 1917 and subsequently served as Governor-General of New Zealand.
- He died in 1935, aged 76.

(Fig. 10.29)

DAVID BEATTY, 1st EARL BEATTY

(Fig. 10.30)

- Admiral of the Fleet David Richard Beatty (1871–1936) was a *navy officer*.
- In 1916, he commanded the 1st Battlecruiser Squadron at the *Battle of Jutland*.
- It was a tactically indecisive engagement, after which his aggressive approach was contrasted with the caution of his commander **Admiral Sir John Jellicoe**.
- Beatty is remembered for his comment at Jutland: '*There seems to be something wrong with our bloody ships today*', after two of his ships exploded.
- Later in the war, he succeeded Jellicoe as Commander-in-Chief of the Grand Fleet, and received the surrender of the German Fleet at the end of the war.
- He then served as First Sea Lord and was involved in negotiating the Washington Naval Treaty (1922).
- He died in 1939, aged 65.

ARTHUR TEDDER, 1st BARON TEDDER

(Fig. 10.31)

- Marshal of the RAF Arthur William Tedder (1890–1967) was an *air force officer*.
- During WW1, he was a squadron commander in the Royal Flying Corps and then served as a senior officer in the RAF.
- During WW2, Tedder was an Air Officer commanding the RAF Middle East Command and directed air operations in the Mediterranean and North Africa.
- Later in the war, he was closely involved in the planning of the invasion of Sicily and Italy.
- He was then appointed Deputy Supreme Commander under **General Eisenhower** (Fig. 10.32).
- After the war, he served as Chief of the Air Staff and in 1948, he was involved in the Berlin Airlift.
- He died in 1967, aged 77.

(Fig. 10.32)

HUGH DOWDING, 1st BARON DOWDING

(Fig. 10.33)

- Air Chief Marshal Hugh Caswall Tremenheere Dowding (1882–1970) was an *air force officer*.
- During WW1, he served as a fighter pilot and then as a commanding officer.
- In WW2, during the *Battle of Britain* (July–Oct. 1940) (Fig. 10.34), he was an Air Officer commanding the RAF Fighter Command. He is generally credited with playing a crucial role in Britain's defence and hence the defeat of Hitler's plan to invade Britain.
- In November 1940, he was unwillingly replaced by **Air Chief Marshal Sholto Douglas** (Fig. 10.35).
- He died in 1970, aged 88.

(Fig. 10.34)    *(Fig. 10.35)*

ARTHUR HARRIS, 1st BARONET

(Fig. 10.36)

- Marshal of the RAF Sir Arthur Travers Harris (1892–1984), commonly known as 'Bomber Harris', was an *air force officer.*
- In WW1, he joined the Royal Flying Corps, in which he remained until the formation of the RAF.
- At the outbreak of WW2, Harris took command of No. 5 Group RAF and in February 1942, he was appointed head of Bomber Command, making the British War Cabinet agree to *'area bombing'* of German cities.
- Harris assisted **Charles Portal** (Fig. 10.37) in carrying out devastating attacks against the German infrastructure and population, including the Bombing of Dresden (Fig. 10.38).
- He died in 1984, aged 92.

(Fig. 10.37)

(Fig. 10.38)

ANDREW CUNNINGHAM, 1st VISCOUNT CUNNINGHAM OF HYNDHOPE

(Fig. 10.39)

- Admiral of the Fleet Andrew Browne Cunningham (1883–1963), nicknamed 'ABC', was a *naval officer*.
- During WW1, he commanded a destroyer and was awarded the DSO and two bars for his actions in the Dardanelles and Baltic.
- In WW2, he served as Commander-in-Chief of the Mediterranean

Fleet and was involved in the attack on *Taranto* (1940) and the *Battle of Cape Matapan* (1941).
- Cunningham controlled the defence of the Mediterranean supply lines through Alexandria, Gibraltar, and the key checkpoint of Malta.
- He also directed naval support for the various major landings in the Western Mediterranean.
- In 1943, he became First Sea Lord, a position he held until his retirement in 1946.
- He then enjoyed several ceremonial positions until he died in 1963, aged 80.

LOUIS MOUNTBATTEN, 1st EARL MOUNTBATTEN OF BURMA

(Fig. 10.40)

- Admiral of the Fleet Louis Francis Albert Mountbatten, born Prince Louis of Battenberg (1900–1979) was a *naval officer* and *Viceroy of India*.
- He was the uncle of Prince Philip, Duke of Edinburgh and the second cousin once removed of Queen Elizabeth 2nd.
- During WW2, he was Supreme Commander of South East Asia Command (1943–1946).
- He was the last Viceroy of India (1947) (Fig. 10.41) and the first Governor-General of independent India (1947–1948).

- From 1954 until 1959, he was First Sea Lord, a position that had been held by his father, **Prince Louis of Battenberg** (Fig. 10.42), some forty years earlier.
- Thereafter, he served as Chief of the Defence Staff until 1965.
- In 1979, aged 79, Mountbatten, his grandson Nicholas, and two others were killed by the Provisional Irish Republic Army.

(Fig. 10.41)    *(Fig. 10.42)*

HAROLD ALEXANDER, 1st EARL ALEXANDER OF TUNIS

(Fig. 10.43)

- Field Marshal Harold Rupert Alexander (1891–1969) was an *army officer* and *governor of Canada*.
- During WW1, he received numerous honours and decorations and was involved in various campaigns across Europe and Asia.

- During WW2, Alexander oversaw the final stages of the evacuation of Dunkirk and subsequently held high-ranking commands in Burma, North Africa, and Italy.
- He was then promoted to Field Marshal and Supreme Allied Commander in the Mediterranean.
- In 1946, he was appointed Governor of Canada and held the post until 1952.
- Alexander retired in 1954 and died in 1969, aged 78.

BERNARD MONTGOMERY, 1st VISCOUNT MONTGOMERY OF ALAMEIN

(Fig. 10.44)

- Field Marshal Bernard Law Montgomery (1887–1976) was an *army officer*.
- In WW1, he was shot through the right lung during the *First Battle of Ypres* (Oct.–Nov. 1914).
- During WW2, from August 1942, he commanded the British 8th Army in the Western Desert, including the *Second Battle of El Alamein* (Fig. 10.45), a turning point in the desert campaign.
- He subsequently commanded the British 8th Army during the

(Fig. 10.45)

(Fig. 10.46)

invasions of Sicily and Italy. He was then in command of all ground forces during Operation Overlord, from the initial landings (Fig. 10.46) until after the *Battle of Normandy* (June 1944).

- He then continued to command of the 21st Army Group for the rest of the campaign in North West Europe. He was the principal Field Commander associated with the failed airborne attempt to bridge the river Rhine at Arnhem and the Allied Rhine crossing.
- On 4th May 1945, he took the German surrender at Luneburg Heath (Fig. 10.47).

(Fig. 10.47)

- After the war, he became Commander-in-Chief of the British Army of the Rhine and then Chief of the Imperial General Staff (1946–48).
- He then served as Deputy Supreme Commander of NATO in Europe until his retirement in 1958.
- He died in 1973, aged 86.

ARCHIBALD WAVELL, 1st EARL WAVELL

(Fig. 10.48)

- Field Marshal Archibald Percival Wavell (1883–1950) was an *army officer* and *Viceroy* of *India.*
- He served in the *Second Boer War* and during WW1, he was wounded in the *Second Battle of Ypres* (April–May 1915).
- During WW2, he served initially as Commander-in-Chief of the Middle East.
- Wavell led British forces to victory over the Italians in western Egypt and in eastern Libya during *Operation Compass* (December 1940), but then he was defeated by the Germans in the Western Desert Campaign (April 1941).
- Between July 1941 and June 1943, he served as Commander-in-Chief in India and then he became Viceroy of India until his retirement in February 1947.
- He died in 1950, aged 67.